COUNTRIES OF THE WORLD

Jamaica

Gareth Stevens Publishing
A WORLD ALMANAC EDUCATION GROUP COMPANY

About the Author: Kerry-Ann Morris is a historian, teacher, and freelance writer living in Jamaica. She is also a graduate student at the University of the West Indies, where she is pursuing a master of philosophy degree in history.

Written by
KERRY-ANN MORRIS

Edited by
KRISINDER MUKHTIAR KAUR

Edited in the U.S. by
JOANN EARLY MACKEN

Designed by
BENSON TAN

Picture research by
SUSAN JANE MANUEL

First published in North America in 2003 by
Gareth Stevens Publishing
A World Almanac Education Group Company
330 West Olive Street, Suite 100
Milwaukee, Wisconsin 53212 USA

Please visit our web site at:
www.garethstevens.com
For a free color catalog describing
Gareth Stevens Publishing's list of high-quality
books and multimedia programs, call
1-800-542-2595 (USA) or 1-800-387-3178 (Canada).
Gareth Stevens Publishing's fax: (414) 332-3567.

© **TIMES MEDIA PRIVATE LIMITED 2003**
Originated and designed by
Times Editions
An imprint of Times Media Private Limited
A member of the Times Publishing Group
Times Centre, 1 New Industrial Road
Singapore 536196
http://www.timesone.com.sg/te

Library of Congress Cataloging-in-Publication Data
Morris, Kerry-Ann.
Jamaica/ by Kerry-Ann Morris.
p. cm. — (Countries of the world)
Summary: An overview of Jamaica, including information on its geography, history, government, social life and customs, and relationship with the United States.
Includes bibliographical references and index.
ISBN 0-8368-2364-8 (lib. bdg.)
1. Jamaica—Juvenile literature. [1. Jamaica.]
I. Title. II. Countries of the world (Milwaukee, Wis.)
F1868.2.M67   2003
972.92—dc21   2003041784

Printed in Singapore

1 2 3 4 5 6 7 8 9 06 05 04 03

PICTURE CREDITS

Agence France Presse: 76, 83, 85
Art Directors and Trip Photographic Library: 7, 8, 16, 17, 18 (bottom), 25 (top), 26, 27 (top), 30 (bottom), 37, 41 (both), 49, 55, 56, 57, 58, 59, 62, 63, 65, 75, 78, 81
Jan Butchofsky/Houserstock: 1, 25 (bottom)
Camera Press: 48, 77
Steve Cohen/Houserstock: 9, 44, 66 (top)
Focus Team — Italy: Cover,10, 20, 51, 67
Haga Library: 4, 24, 40, 60, 61, 68, 72, 73
David G. Houser/Houserstock: 33 (top)
Hulton Archives/Getty Images: 11, 13, 14, 15 (bottom), 27 (bottom), 33 (bottom), 39, 46 (both), 52, 53, 54, 84
Hutchison Library: 18 (top), 29, 50
Kay Shaw Photo: 42
Jason Laure: 69
North Wind Picture Archives: 47, 64, 70, 71
Lynn Seldon: 31, 34, 43, 45, 80
David Simson: 5, 6, 12, 19, 21, 22, 23, 28, 32, 35, 36, 38, 66 (bottom), 74, 79, 82
Topham Picturepoint: 15 (top)
Travel Ink: 30 (top), 91

Digital Scanning by Superskill Graphics Pte Ltd

Contents

AN OVERVIEW OF JAMAICA

Jamaica's motto "Out of Many, One People" attests to the diverse nature of this small Caribbean island. From its flora and fauna to its people and culture, Jamaica's diversity is well known and held in great esteem around the world. In its short history, this small island, nestled in the Greater Antilles of the Caribbean, has endured many years of struggle, political controversy, and economic uncertainty. Jamaican artists, businesspeople, students, politicians, and athletes have all contributed to the creation of this powerful Caribbean nation. The people of Jamaica are proud of their rich cultural heritage, and today, there are many Jamaican communities in other parts of the world.

Opposite: **In the resort area of Negril, at the western edge of Jamaica, beach huts built on cliffs overlook the ocean.**

Below: **At this festival market in Fern Gully, in the parish of St. Ann, local Jamaican handcrafted goods are sold.**

THE FLAG OF JAMAICA

The current flag of Jamaica was unveiled at the stroke of midnight on August 6, 1962, the day Jamaica gained its independence. A gold saltire, or diagonal cross, divides the flag into four triangles. The color gold symbolizes wealth and sunlight. The triangles on either side, known as hoist (left) and fly (right), are black. The color black represents the hardships Jamaicans have encountered in the past and may face in the future. The top and bottom triangles are green. The color green stands for the plentiful agricultural resources of the country and the hope of its people.

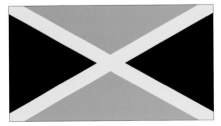

Geography

Jamaica is the third-largest island in the Greater Antilles, which is a chain of islands that form the northern boundary of the Caribbean Sea. Other islands of the Greater Antilles are Cuba, Puerto Rico, and Hispaniola, which contains Haiti and the Dominican Republic. Jamaica lies 90 miles (145 kilometers) south of Cuba and 100 miles (161 km) west of Haiti. These countries are Jamaica's two nearest neighbors.

Jamaica has an area of 4,244 square miles (10,992 square km) and is the largest Caribbean island with an English-speaking population. The island measures 146 miles (235 km) from east to west and is 50 miles wide (80 km) from St. Ann's Bay to Portland Point, its widest point. Jamaica's terrain is very mountainous. The island is actually the tip of a submerged mountain that is part of a range that includes Hispaniola, Puerto Rico, the string of smaller islands running south to Trinidad, and the Venezuelan mountains bracketing the Gulf of Paria. Christopher Columbus, one of the first Europeans to visit the island, described it as "the fairest island eyes have beheld."

Below: **Montego Bay is in the parish of St. James. Christopher Columbus was one of the first Europeans to visit this area.**

Left: **Many rare and exotic plants can be found in the forests of the Blue Mountains.**

THE BLUE MOUNTAINS

The world-famous Jamaica Blue Mountain coffee beans are grown on the slopes of the Blue Mountain range at elevations of up to 5,000 feet (1,524 m).
(A Closer Look, page 44)

Mountains

Mountains dominate the Jamaican landscape, with nearly half of the island measuring 1,000 feet (305 meters) above sea level. The main group of mountains extends from east to west along the island's middle and forms what has been described as the "backbone of Jamaica." Extending north and south from the central range are smaller ranges, from which smaller spurs branch out in various directions. As a result, the Jamaican terrain is characterized by ridges and valleys.

Jamaica's complex system of mountains can be divided into three main groups: eastern, western, and central. The eastern group consists of the Blue Mountains and the John Crow Mountains, while Dolphin Head, a proposed national park, is at the center of the western group. The central group extends from Stony Hill in St. Andrew to the Cockpit Country in Trelawny.

Of the Caribbean islands, Jamaica has the greatest number of botanical gardens, which were established during the English colonial era to propogate exotic fruit crops introduced from other English colonies. Jamaica is also home to two national parks and some wilderness areas, which are protected by law. The two national parks are the Blue Mountains-John Crow National Park and Montego Bay Marine Park.

THE GREAT PORT ROYAL EARTHQUAKE

The island of Jamaica is vulnerable to severe earthquakes. The Europeans in Jamaica were the first to keep records of such disasters. The Port Royal earthquake of 1692 is an example of one of Jamaica's biggest earthquake disasters.
(A Closer Look, page 50)

Climatic Conditions

Located between the equator and the tropic of Cancer, Jamaica has a subtropical climate. Altitude, however, causes temperatures to vary widely from region to region on the island. The capital city, Kingston, has an annual average temperature of 90° Fahrenheit (32° Celsius).

Jamaica experiences two rainy seasons, during May and from October to November. The island receives an annual average of about 82 inches (208 centimeters) of rain, and more rain is known to fall on Jamaica's northern coast than on its southern coast.

In Jamaica, the period from June 1 to November 30 is known as the hurricane season. Although Jamaica lies within the Caribbean's "hurricane belt," relatively few hurricanes have blown through the island. Hurricane Gilbert was the last major hurricane to strike Jamaica; it devastated the island on September 12, 1988.

Above: **Rio Grande is in the parish of Portland. Most rivers in Jamaica are not navigable because of the country's very mountainous terrain. The island's largest navigable river is the Black River, which flows for 44 miles (71 km) in the parish of St. Elizabeth.**

Flora and Fauna

Jamaica is home to more than 3,000 species of flowering plants, including 220 species of orchids. Jamaica is also renowned for having 550 species of ferns. The island has few mammal species, and among them are the mongoose and the Jamaican hutia. The mongoose is the most common mammal in Jamaica, while the Jamaican hutia is an endangered species. Also known as the coney, the Jamaican hutia is a large, brown rodent that resembles a guinea pig. Animal life on the island also includes as many as twenty-three species of bats, twenty-five species of frogs, thirty species of lizards, and 256 bird species, including the white owl, commonly called *patoo* (PAH-too), and the Jamaica vulture, commonly called "John Crow." The streamertail hummingbird, or "Doctor Bird," as it is known to the locals, is Jamaica's national bird. Wild hogs live in the forests of the John Crow and Blue mountains. Coral reefs and more than 700 species of fish make up much of Jamaican marine life.

FERN GULLY

Many different varieties and sizes of exotic ferns grow in Fern Gully in the parish of St. Ann. Along the 3-mile (5 km) canyon, the vegetation forms a thick, cooling canopy over the road.

Below: The island's crocodile population is found in wetlands and mangrove swamps along the southern coast, most notably in the Font Hill Reserve, Black River Morass, and Long Bay.

History

The European Colonizers

Jamaica's recent history began with European interest in finding another route to the spice centers of Asia. In 1492, explorer Christopher Columbus reached the island of Hispaniola and began the European settlement and colonization of the Caribbean islands. Columbus arrived in Jamaica in 1494, when he made his second voyage to the New World. Spaniards built a colony in Jamaica in 1509, but they mainly used the island as a supply base for conquering the Americas.

The Spanish were concerned with conquering and settling as many overseas territories as possible and spreading Christianity to the people of conquered lands. In Jamaica, the Spanish enslaved the native *Taino* (tah-EE-no) people to work on plantations. A combination of European diseases, hard labor, harsh treatment, and outright murder wiped out the Taino population within a few decades.

ENGLISH CONQUERORS

In 1655, the English captured Jamaica under the leadership of Admiral William Penn and General Robert Venables. The English began to destroy the Spanish capital, St. Jago de la Vega, which later became known as Spanish Town. Jamaica remained a colony of England for 307 years, gaining its independence in 1962.

BUCCANEERS AND PIRATES

Notorious buccaneers and fierce pirates were once a common sight in Jamaica. They used Jamaica as a base to carry out their activities from the sixteenth to the eighteenth century.
(*A Closer Look*, page 46)

Left: European architecture is a feature of several government buildings in Spanish Town, Jamaica.

White and Immigrant Contract Labor

In the early 1700s, before African slavery became recognized as an alternative to the lost Taino labor, the English depended on indentured, or contract, laborers from England and the surrounding Caribbean islands. These laborers worked on plantations, in sugar mills, and as domestics. They were required to serve a contract period of five years with their employers. Many of them were ill-treated. Because they were expensive to import, employers eventually found it unprofitable to hire them.

After the emancipation of thousands of slaves in Jamaica in 1838, sugar planters found it more difficult to find labor. To rectify the problem, the Colonial Office in London, which looked after the affairs of English colonies in the West Indies, allowed the importation of contract immigrant labor from other parts of the world. Labor was thus sought from other countries, such as China, India, Trinidad and Tobago, and British Guiana.

Above: **This illustration shows immigrant indentured laborers picking cotton in the fields of eighteenth-century Jamaica.**

THE MAROONS

The Maroons are the descendants of runaway slaves who fought for their freedom against the English from the seventeenth to the nineteenth century. The town of Accompong in the parish of St. Elizabeth is one of several Maroon settlements in Jamaica.
(A Closer Look, page 60)

The 1865 Morant Bay Rebellion

After the emancipation of the slaves and economic changes in Europe, Jamaica's economy declined. Social conditions were very poor. The black population suffered the most from a drop in sugar prices, failure of plantations, unemployment, racial discrimination, and drought.

When some peasants sent an appeal to the Queen of England for help, her reply did not satisfy them. On August 12, 1865, Paul Bogle, a prosperous small farmer and ordained deacon of the Baptist Church, led a group of peasants from Stony Gut in St. Thomas parish to Spanish Town in St. Catherine to see the governor, Edward John Eyre. He refused to see them. The frustration of the peasants grew until it erupted on October 11, 1865. Violence broke out during a march on the Morant Bay courthouse led by Bogle. The courthouse was burned, and a number of white people died in the flames.

The governor sent out his troops to find the rebels and had them severely punished. George William Gordon, the son of a slave woman, a member of the Legislative Assembly, and a supporter of the poor for many years, was arrested, tried, and hanged for his alleged involvement in the rebellion, even though no evidence proved that he organized it. Paul Bogle was also found guilty and hanged.

A CROWN COLONY

After the rebellion, the governing power of the island was changed. The elected governing body, the Legislative Assembly, in which the planters had more say in the running of the country, was disbanded. Jamaica became a crown colony governed only by England.

THE NATIONAL HEROES

The Order of National Hero is the highest honorary award presented by the Jamaican govenment to outstanding Jamaicans. A National Hero is given the title "Right Excellent." Jamaica has named six National Heroes.

(A Closer Look, page 62)

Trade Unions and Political Parties

At the beginning of the twentieth century, Jamaican workers first began to organize themselves into groups to protect their own interests. Such unions were badly needed because the workers' conditions were very poor, and they lacked organizations through which they could discuss problems and complaints with their employers.

The first officially recognized trade union in Jamaica was the Bustamante Industrial Trade Union (BITU), which was established in January 1939 and led by Alexander Bustamante. With the formation of trade unions, middle-class politicians also began to demand self-government, higher wages, and better social services for the workers. These demands resulted in the formation of political parties. The first was the People's National Party (PNP), headed by Norman Manley. Initially, the PNP and BITU had an alliance, but Bustamante later broke from the PNP to form his own party, the Jamaica Labor Party (JLP). On December 12, 1944, Jamaica was granted universal adult suffrage. This meant that all citizens of Jamaica who were aged eighteen and above could vote for the government of their choice. Elections were then held using this system for the first time, and the Jamaica Labor Party won.

Below: **Queen Elizabeth II** *(front row, middle)* **poses for a picture with the members of the Commonwealth of Nations. The Jamaican prime minister at the time, Alexander Bustamante, stands directly behind the queen. The photograph was taken on September 13, 1962, at a banquet at Buckingham Palace.**

Achieving Independence

In the early years of World War II, protests against the crown colony system continued strongly in Jamaica. Middle-class politicians and common laborers were unhappy with the less-than-equal opportunities given to locals concerning their participation in the running of their own country.

In 1958, at the suggestion of the British government, Jamaica and other British islands in the Caribbean formed the West Indies Federation within the Commonwealth of Nations, an association of fifty-four independent countries that were formerly colonies of Great Britain. In 1959, Jamaica was granted full self-government, and Norman Manley, the PNP leader, became the prime minister of the nation.

In 1961, Jamaicans voted against remaining in the West Indies Federation. Jamaica withdrew from the federation and was granted independence on August 6, 1962. Elections were held in that same year, and the leader of the JLP, Alexander Bustamante, became the prime minister of independent Jamaica. The island remained a member of the Commonwealth of Nations.

CARIBBEAN FEDERATION

The idea of joining the West Indies Federation was not well supported in Jamaica. Jamaicans feared that the less prosperous members would be an economic burden and that their country, the most populous, did not have adequate representation.

Below: **Alexander Bustamante** *(far left)* **and Norman Manley** *(far right)* **shake hands with members of the British Colonial Office after the final session of the Jamaica Independence Conference in 1962.**

Mary Jane Seacole (1805–1881)

Regarded as the "Florence Nightingale of Jamaica," Mary Jane Seacole dedicated her life to healing the sick and comforting the injured. Born in Jamaica, she received no formal training in nursing but was taught traditional healing methods by her mother. She became a highly skilled nurse. In 1850, when Jamaica and other Caribbean islands experienced their first outbreak of cholera, Mary Seacole prepared a medicine to cure those who were suffering from the disease and also took it to Panama and Cuba. Although she faced racial discrimination, Mary was determined to volunteer her services. She received three medals for the medical assistance she provided during the Crimean War.

Mary Jane Seacole

Sir Alexander Bustamante (1884–1977)

Fondly remembered as the "champion of Jamaica's working class," Sir Alexander Bustamante was Jamaica's first prime minister. He set up the first trade union in Jamaica and was well-loved by the Jamaican masses. He was affectionately called "Busta," or "chief," by his political followers. He retired from Jamaican politics in 1967 and was later appointed a National Hero for his contributions toward freeing Jamaica from colonial rule.

Dr. Thomas P. Lecky (1904–1994)

Dr. Thomas P. Lecky developed Jamaica's own tropical dairy breed. Born in the parish of Portland, he grew up on a small farm, where he developed a love for animals. He studied agriculture at McGill University and animal husbandry at Ontario Agricultural College, where his studies showed that the method of breeding cattle used in Jamaica was not the best. He went on to develop a new breed of cattle he called the "Jamaica Hope." For the first time, there was a tropical breed of cows that could give up to 20,000 pounds (9,072 kilograms) of milk in a year. Since the breed was created, it has been in high demand in many other countries. Dr. Lecky died in May 1994. The legacy of his work is still felt today, especially among small cattle farmers.

Sir Alexander Bustamante

Government and the Economy

The Political Structure

Jamaica inherited its political institutions from Britain. Jamaica is a constitutional parliamentary democracy within the Commonwealth of Nations. Its government consists of executive, legislative, and judicial branches. The executive branch includes the governor general, locally referred to as the "GG," who represents the titular head of state, Queen Elizabeth II of England, but has few governing powers. Executive power resides with a cabinet that is led by the prime minister and responsible to the parliament. The members of the cabinet are responsible for such ministries as finance, agriculture, and education. Ministers are members of the parliament. The parliament consists of the Senate and the House of Representatives. Senators are appointed, but representatives are elected. Elections must be held at least once every five years. The judicial branch consists of the Court of Appeal and courts of original jurisdiction.

Below: **This government building is in Spanish Town, which served as Jamaica's capital from 1662 to 1872.**

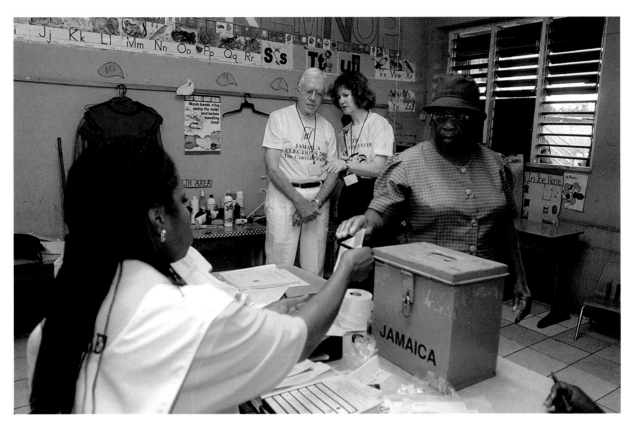

Local Government

The parliament, sometimes called the Central Government, has its headquarters in Kingston, the capital city. Parish councils make up the local government of Jamaica. Parish council members are elected every three years. Sometimes, the parliament chooses to extend the number of years that these members serve.

To carry out their work, the parish councils receive money from the central government, collected as parish rates and trade licenses or paid as grants. The chief work of the parish councils is to look after the local interests within the parishes in connection with matters such as the care of the poor, public health sanitation, garbage collection, street cleaning, and maintenance of roads, parks, and markets.

Political Parties and Elections

Today, two major political parties dominate the politics of the country. They are the Jamaica Labor Party (JLP) and the People's National Party (PNP). The most recent nationwide elections were conducted in Jamaica in 2002. The PNP, led by Prime Minister P. J. Patterson, won the elections for the fourth consecutive time.

Above: **A woman** *(right)* **votes in the Jamaican general elections held in 2002. All Jamaican citizens are entitled to vote when they reach eighteen years of age.**

Economy

Jamaica's economy is highly developed compared to those of most Caribbean countries. The country has an active stock market; many international banks; a large, skilled workforce, and a relatively broad-based economy. The economy, however, depends on imported consumer goods and raw materials that exceed the country's earnings from tourism, bauxite, sugar, and bananas. Jamaica imports more goods than it exports, so it cannot pay for imported goods. The island is troubled by massive foreign debt and faces an acute balance-of-payments crisis. Jamaica also suffers from high inflation and increasing unemployment rates.

Jamaica's leading industries include agriculture, tourism, mining, bananas, and fishing. Agriculture is the main industry of the country. The chief cash crops are sugar, bananas, citrus, cocoa, and coconuts. Jamaica is also the world's leading source of pimento, also called allspice. Agriculture and tourism are the country's most important sources of employment. Jamaica is also the world's third-largest producer of bauxite and processed alumina. Bauxite is the ore from which the metal aluminum is produced. Alumina, the refined form of bauxite, makes aluminum when combined with electricity. The United States, the United Kingdom, the European Union, and Canada are Jamaica's main trading partners.

Above: This picture shows a nursery where young banana plants are carefully grown. Most of Jamaica's banana plantations are found on the eastern section of the island.

"KING" SUGAR

Sugar was introduced to the West Indies by explorer Christopher Columbus in the sixteenth century. Toward the seventeenth century, Jamaica became a highly successful producer and exporter of sugar.
(*A Closer Look, page 54*)

Left: These flight attendants are from Air Jamaica airlines, which was formed in 1969 and is now an important facet of the Jamaican tourist industry.

Transportation

The two main ways of getting around in Jamaica are by road and by air. The island has two international airports. The Norman Manley International Airport in Kingston is used mostly for business and local travel. The Sangster International Airport near Montego Bay is close to the main resorts and is used mostly by tourists. In addition, four domestic airports, or aerodromes, serve Jamaican travelers and visitors: Tinson Pen, in Kingston; Ken Jones, near Port Antonio; Negril, near Negril Point; and Boscobel, near Ocho Rios. The national railway service has been out of service for some time now, but efforts are under way to restore it.

Below: **Jamaica's public transportation system is monitored by the Jamaica Urban Transit Company (JUTC).**

Primary Occupations

Jamaican citizens are employed in a variety of different occupations; approximately 1.13 million people make up the workforce. In 2000, 18 percent of Jamaicans worked in the industrial sector, 21 percent in the agricultural sector, and 61 percent in the services sector. A growing number of Jamaicans are involved in the field of information technology, a sector that has the full financial support of the government.

TOURISM

Tourism is Jamaica's most vital industry. The island is one of the top eight small-island destinations in the world.
(A Closer Look, page 72)

People and Lifestyle

In 2002, the total Jamaican population was estimated at 2,680,029, with about 680,000 living in the capital city, Kingston. At least another two million Jamaicans live abroad. The country's motto — "Out of Many, One People" — attests to the diverse nature of the people who make up its population. During the days of slavery, tens of thousands of West Africans and hundreds of Europeans came to the island forcibly and voluntarily.

After emancipation of the slaves in 1838, more people of different cultures came to the island. These were the Europeans, Chinese, and East Indians. The majority of these new people remained on the island and contributed significantly to the diversity of the Jamaican population today. Unique religions, music, food, and art forms have developed on the island and, in some cases, spread overseas to influence other cultures. Today, there are Jamaican immigrant populations in many countries all over the world.

KINGSTON

A vibrant city, Kingston is the commercial center of Jamaica. Many government bodies and boards are also located in Kingston.

(A Closer Look, page 56)

Below: Colorful street markets such as this one dot the streets of Montego Bay.

Jamaica's population today reflects the island's history and the diverse groups of people who traveled there. About 90.9 percent of the Jamaican population is of African descent, and 7.3 percent is of mixed parentage. Several other groups are minorities on the island. People of East Indian background make up 1.3 percent of the population, 0.2 percent are Chinese, 0.2 percent are white, and the remainder are Jews and Middle Easterners. The island has a number of poor whites, the descendants of Welsh, Scottish, Irish, and German indentured laborers who arrived after emancipation. Jews have a long history in Jamaica. They first arrived in significant numbers during the Spanish colonial period, when they were forced to flee the inquisition in Spain. Under the constitution of Jamaica, all racial groups are entitled to equal status and opportunities and given the right to vote in state elections. Such rules help prevent racial discrimination in Jamaica.

Above: **These two girls reflect the cultural diversity that can be found all over the island. Children of different races study, play, and interact with one another every day.**

THE SLAVE TRADE

Thousands of Africans came to Jamaica as slaves starting in the middle of the sixteenth century. Many of them were from the western region of Africa.
(A Closer Look, page 70)

Rural and Urban Communities

The population of Jamaica is centered around the Kingston area. Kingston, the capital city, is the seat of government and the hub of industry, commerce, and culture for the whole island. The city has numerous suburbs and is steadily expanding as a residential area and industrial district. Many people reside in Kingston in order to live closer to their jobs. Others commute to work every day from other sections of the island.

Those who live in the rural communities depend on agriculture to earn a living. They either own their own farms or are employed on the farms of others. They grow crops such as bananas, plantains, and cassava on these farms. Employment in the rural communities is also found in tourist areas such as Ocho Rios and St. Ann and in other industries such as mining.

Poverty is a serious problem among Jamaican families living in rural areas. It is estimated that the people in one-fourth of rural Jamaican households live in poverty. This percentage is significantly higher than the poverty rate in urban Jamaica.

POLLUTION IN THE KINGSTON HARBOR

Jamaica's major shipping activities take place at the Kingston Harbor. In recent years, however, the Kingston Harbor has become highly polluted.
(A Closer Look, page 64)

Below: This shack is in Cockpit Country. Besides housing problems, parts of rural Jamaica also suffer from a lack of adequate educational facilities as well as public services.

Family Life

Many different types of families live on the island, including the traditional nuclear family with two parents and children; the single parent family with either a father or mother looking after a child or children; the extended family of parents, grandparents, children, cousins, aunts, and uncles; and the family that is not related by blood but by circumstances.

Many parents, mostly mothers, emigrate to the United States or England to work. They may leave their children under the care of guardians if family members are not around to look after them. Some parents send items to their children such as clothes and school supplies, which are stored in wooden barrels. These children are often referred to as "barrel children" because they have to collect these barreled items at the customs department.

In recent years, the number of single mothers in Jamaica has been on the rise. Many of these single mothers are teenagers. There are also many men who have more than one family. Most fathers in Jamaica play a smaller role in taking care of their children than mothers do.

Above: **Jamaican families often spend Sundays together at home after their visit to the local church.**

LEGENDS AND FOLKTALES

Many interesting Jamaican folktales are originally from parts of Africa. They were brought to Jamaica by African slaves and have become a part of Jamaica's rich heritage.
(A Closer Look, page 58)

Education

In the past, education in Jamaica was a luxury that only the rich could afford. Wealthy planters sent their children to private schools while the poorer section of society received only basic religious schooling. Since then, the education system has been through many reforms, moving beyond primary schooling to more advanced education. Now, 85 percent of Jamaicans age fifteen and above are literate. Efforts are under way to increase this literacy rate across the island.

Jamaican children begin school at age three, spending an average of two years in kindergarten and six years in primary school. At age eleven or twelve, children enter high school, where they spend five years. They may spend an additional two years if they attend sixth form. In sixth form, students have the option to further their education by applying for entry to one of the universities in the country. The University of the West Indies (UWI), the University of Technology (Utech), and Northern Caribbean University (NCU), as well as foreign universities such as Nova Southeastern University and Florida State University, offer degree programs to Jamaicans.

Below: Jamaican students enjoy their recess break. A number of changes have been made to the Jamaican education system in the past few years. For example, previously, primary school students had to take a Common Entrance Exam in order to gain entry into secondary school. This exam has been replaced with a better program known as The National Assessment Program.

Women in Jamaica

Above and *below:*
**Women in Jamaica
take on varied roles
in Jamaican society.**

Women play many important roles in Jamaican society. They often are the heads of their households and the only parents in their homes. They also outnumber men in the labor force, and they dominate a few particular job sectors. For instance, teaching, once a male-dominated occupation, is now predominantly female in composition. The percentage of women in decision-making positions in the Jamaican government, however, is still quite low. In rural Jamaica, women face greater difficulty in obtaining jobs than men do.

More women than men attend higher-level institutions such as the University of the West Indies. There also is a higher percentage of literate adult females than males in Jamaica; 86 percent of Jamaican women can read and write, compared to only 74.1 percent of Jamaican men.

Jamaican women are known widely for their independence. In relationships, they often maintain their own separate property and have their own sources of income. This can be a source of conflict because a large percentage of Jamaican men expect women to play subservient roles. They may feel threatened by women who are educated and independent.

Religion

Jamaica is said to have the greatest number of churches per square mile (square km) of any country in the world. More than 65 percent of the Jamaican population is Christian, with a wide variety of Christian denominations represented in the country. Christianity, in the form of Roman Catholicism, was introduced to Jamaica by Spanish settlers in the sixteenth century. The Spanish were unsuccessful in converting the local Taino population. Later, when the English arrived in Jamaica, they brought Protestantism to the island. Today, the church serves as an important social center in Jamaican communities.

A vast majority of Christian Jamaicans are Protestants, who make up 61.3 percent of the country's population. Over 21 percent of Jamaicans are followers of the Church of God, and they form the largest Protestant group in the country. Other significant Protestant groups include the Baptists, Anglicans, Seventh-Day Adventists, and Pentecostalists. Only about 4 percent of Jamaicans are Roman Catholic.

Other religions, such as Judaism, Islam, and Hinduism, as well as the homegrown religious group and popular movement, Rastafarianism, are also present in Jamaica. Followers of non-

Below: **The North Street Cathedral in Kingston is one of the many Roman Catholic churches in Jamaica.**

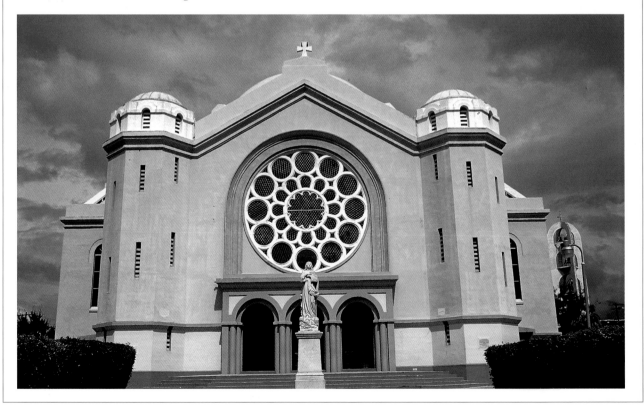

Left: **This woman is a Kumina priestess. Kumina is a religious cult of African origins. Its rituals involve bands of people dancing in a circle to the sound of drumbeats and chanting. The ritual climaxes with the dancers seemingly possessed by spirits. In this state, they give messages, warnings, and revelations of future events.**

RASTAFARIANS

A religion created in twentieth-century Jamaica, Rastafarianism professes that Haile Selassie *(below)*, the former emperor of Ethiopia, is the Black Messiah and king of all Africa.

(A Closer Look, Page 66)

Christian religions, which include traditional African beliefs and voodoo, or black magic, practices, account for nearly 35 percent of the country's population.

Kumina (koo-MEE-nah) and *Pocomania* (poh-koh-MAY-nee-ah) are traditional Jamaican religions with deep African roots. Both religions are heavily animistic, which means that followers believe that spirits reside in natural objects, such as trees and rocks, and that these spirits can be persuaded to do good or evil with worship.

Although most Jamaicans practice Christian beliefs and attend church services, there are some who still hold onto the belief in the local *obeah* (oh-BEE-ah) man. Obeah men are practitioners who claim to be able to invoke the assistance of spirits and ghosts, locally called "duppies." Many Jamaicans regard obeah as black magic.

Language and Literature

Language

Jamaica's official language is English. In reality, however, Jamaica is a bilingual society with English widely understood but not regularly used in everyday conversation. Jamaicans speak a creolized version of English called Jamaican *patois* (pa-TWAH), which evolved from the mixture of the Creole English of the British colonizers, the African language of the slaves, and Spanish and Portuguese terms.

In the past, the use of Jamaican patois was discouraged because it did not follow standard English. Many Jamaican schools prioritized the teaching of standard English over Jamaican patois. As a result, Jamaican children who were raised in families that spoke Jamaican patois at home faced difficulties in adopting standard English. The negative attitude towards Jamaican patois has declined over the years, and it has now been recognized as the island's second language. There has been much research into its structure at the University of the West Indies.

Below: **Most Jamaican newspapers are written in standard British English and do not use the local dialect.**

Literature

The independence movement of the 1960s opened the gates to greater recognition of literature created by Jamaican writers. Freed from the social restrictions of the colonial period, Jamaican writers expressed their love of their country, as well as their hopes and aspirations for their new society, with creative use of English and the once-forbidden Jamaican patois. Literature took on a more local flavor with poems, stories, and books about Jamaican life and the characters that make up that life. Synonymous with this movement is Louise Bennett-Coverley, who captured the very heart of everyday Jamaican life through her poems and short stories. With much difficulty, she was also successful in making Jamaican patois acceptable to its own speakers as well as within other circles outside of Jamaica.

Other Jamaican writers address anti-colonial themes in their books. They express the necessity for Jamaicans to protest against the social ills of the colonial period. Claude McKay, Vic Reid, Newille Dawes, Andrew Salkey, and Roger Mais are some of Jamaica's other well known writers.

Above: **The literature of many Jamaican writers and poets is incorporated in the curriculum of most Jamaican schools.**

CULTURAL ICON OF JAMAICA

Louise Bennett-Coverley has received many awards for her contributions to Jamaican literature. She is well known for her stories about Anancy, a cunning spider who often outwits his enemies.
(A Closer Look, page 48)

Arts

Jamaica has a vibrant artistic culture, which is especially apparent in Kingston. Since 1962, when the country became independent, art forms, such as music, dance, drama, and the fine arts, have all taken on a distinct Jamaican flavor and flourished.

Visual Arts

Jamaica's art forms have evolved out of the beliefs and rituals of the society as well as the country's prevailing social, political, and economic circumstances. This evolution has resulted in a kaleidoscope of artistic creations. The National Gallery is the starting point for any understanding of Jamaican art. It houses the nation's largest collection of historical and contemporary art.

A pivotal figure in the creation of a distinct Jamaican art form was Edna Manley, wife of former prime minister and National Hero Norman Washington Manley. Edna Manley was a founding member of the art school in Kingston that bears her name. Many of her sculptures grace the walls and hallways of organizations and institutions such as the University of the West Indies.

Jamaica's visual arts also include ceramics, or pottery. Of all the artistic activities in Jamaica, pottery has the longest and most consistent history. It began with the Taino people, who used the island's red clay to make various kinds of earthenware, including cooking vessels.

Above: **A professional potter demonstrates the art of pottery.**

Left: **The National Gallery in Kingston has many works from Jamaica's most distinguished potter, Cecil Baugh. He has earned local and international acclaim as a potter and is well respected locally. He taught others the fine art of pottery at the Edna Manley School of the Visual Arts, and his ceramics and pottery pieces adorn many homes, offices, and public buildings.**

Dance

Jamaicans love to dance. Dance in Jamaican society has roots in Africa and Europe and some East Indian influence as well. Performed dance can be broadly classified as traditional or modern. Traditional dance is heavily African in influence. Many earlier dance forms have lost their social or religious purposes and are mostly revived in performances. Examples of these traditional dance forms are Myal, Kumina, Pocomania, Revival, Quadrille, and Maypole. Pocomania is still performed during religious meetings. Modern dance has an easily recognizable Jamaican style that is heavily influenced by traditional forms and embraces contemporary U.S. techniques as well as European classical ballet.

Fundamental to the recognition of traditional dance forms and the establishment of the modern dance movement in Jamaica is the National Dance Theatre Company (NDTC). It was formed in 1962 by Rex Nettleford and Eddy Thomas. Several other smaller dance companies are L'Acadco, Movements, and The Company. The University of West Indies also has a dance group.

Above: **Many colorful dance performances such as the one shown above are organized for tourists visiting Jamaica to showcase the rich dance heritage of the island.**

Theater

Theater is another vibrant aspect of Jamaica's culture. At one time, Jamaica's performing arts could be divided into two separate types. The first type was the standard theater that included plays by William Shakespeare, operettas, comedies, and pantomimes. These plays were primarily intended for upper class Jamaicans. The second type included folk performances, such as ring games, singing, acting, and dancing, that were enjoyed and supported by urban and peasant people. These two forms eventually merged by the end of the nineteenth century to create a distinct Jamaican theater movement, in which writers skillfully employed both English and Jamaican patois to suit their dramatic purposes.

Several theater groups in Jamaica also use the performing arts as a medium to address serious social problems in Jamaica. The ASHE Performing Arts Ensemble, founded in 1993, is made up mainly of young Jamaicans who put on musicals and dance performances. The group also is involved in various community-based projects, such as educating young Jamaicans about HIV-AIDS. This group has won local and regional acclaim for its talents in music, dance, and drama.

PANTOMIMES

A pantomime is a type of play that has music and grand theater sets and is usually based on a popular fairy tale or folk legend. In most English pantomimes, the actors do not speak, and words are replaced by various bodily movements and gestures. The Jamaican pantomime originates from the English version but has been modified over the years to include speech and dance.

Below: Kingston is still the center of play production and performance with playhouses such as the famous Ward Theatre shown below.

Left: The maracas and banjo used by the musicians shown here are commonly used by Jamaican folk singers.

Music

The world knows Jamaica for reggae music, but other forms of music on the island have also made Jamaica well known. Additionally, Jamaica's musical forms are evolving, with studios producing dozens of recordings each month. Just like dance and theatre, Jamaica's music can be clearly classified into two groups: traditional music and popular music. Jamaica's traditional music form draws on its rich heritage of folk music introduced by African slaves. Much of this traditional music has been lost because the songs and tunes weren't documented until the twentieth century. Traditional music often complements important observances such as birth, puberty, death, mourning, and thanksgiving.

Jamaican popular music evolved through many forms, including mento, ska, rock steady, and reggae. Reggae music has become the heartbeat of Jamaican music and is easily identified internationally as Jamaican. The most recent form, dancehall, is currently the vogue in Jamaican music. Dancehall has its own culture — music, language, dress, style, and worldview. It is extremely popular among young Jamaicans, and it is also a very profitable business.

REGGAE MUSIC

Reggae artists, such as Bob Marley (*below*), made fans of many people worldwide with their unique brand of music. Hope and freedom were common themes in their songs.

(*A Closer Look, page* 68)

Leisure and Festivals

Festivals and Holidays

There are ten public holidays on Jamaica's calendar, as well as a number of festivals particular to the island, such as the Jamaica Festival and National Heritage Week. Major religious holidays on the Christian calendar are celebrated, but strict adherence to the traditional observance of these days is steadily decreasing in Jamaica. For instance, the Lenten dietary restrictions for Easter are decreasingly observed. In the minds of all Jamaicans, the food most associated with Easter is bun and cheese. The bun is a loaf-shaped spiced bread with dried chopped fruit such as raisins, molasses, and sometimes stout, which is similar to beer.

The Jamaica Festival is an islandwide mixture of competitions and exhibitions in the major areas of the arts — music, dance, literature, speech, fine arts, photography, and culinary arts. Thousands of people, young and old, from individuals to schools and community groups, are involved in preparing for "festival,"

INDEPENDENCE DAY

Jamaica held its first Independence Day celebrations at the National Stadium in Kingston in 1962.
(*A Closer Look, page 52*)

Below: **A folk dance performance by local Jamaican women is one of the activities on Independence Day.**

Above: **Holidays are a great time for Jamaican families to relax and enjoy some time together at home.**

as it is commonly called. Elimination rounds begin at the local levels several months before the national finals, which take place during the last two weeks of July, in time to showcase winners at special concerts and exhibitions during independence celebrations in early August. Emancipation Day is held on August 1, and this marks the date in 1838 when the slaves in Jamaica were officially freed from their masters. Today, many Jamaicans commemorate this landmark event in the history of the Jamaican people with virgils held through the night.

National Heritage Week, which takes place in mid-October, began as the centennial celebration of the 1865 Morant Bay Rebellion. National Heroes Day, part of this week-long celebration, is a public holiday. The observances during National Heritage Week are arranged by an official committee to illustrate different themes from year to year. Awards of excellence are presented at the governor-general's residence in Kingston. In 2002, 129 awards were given to people from all sections of Jamaican society.

Sporting Events and Pastime Activities

Sports are a major part of Jamaica's leisure time. Sporting events such as football (soccer), cricket, basketball, and netball are often played after work, after school, and even during break periods at school. There are also islandwide competitions at all levels of the educational system, from primary schools to universities. One example of organized sports for youths is the Interscholastic School Sports Association (ISSA) Boys' and Girls' Championships, which are held every year with competitions in track-and-field events. In 2002, Jamaica hosted the World Junior Championships, in which athletes from many countries across the world competed in track-and-field events.

Football is a very popular and well-funded sport in Jamaica. The Jamaica Football Federation (JFF) is responsible for the football program of the island and for maintaining the national team, the "Reggae Boyz." In 1998, for the first time, Jamaica qualified for the World Cup soccer finals. The Jamaican women's netball team, called the "Sunshine Girls," is among the highest-ranked teams in the world.

NETBALL

The game of netball is a team sport in which two teams compete against each other in a specially marked court. Each team has seven members. The game resembles basketball in that the ultimate aim is to score points by throwing the ball into the basket mounted on a goal post. Slightly different rules, however, govern when netball players run and jump, as well as how they pass the ball during the game.

Below: **Playing beach soccer is a favorite pastime of Jamaicans young and old.**

Above: **This sculpture by Alvin Marriott, called** *The Athlete,* **stands near the National Stadium in Kingston.**

Adult club competitions are organized across and between parishes and within special interest groups, such as private sector companies. Other pastime activities, such as horse racing and dominoes, cut across all class and income boundaries. Whatever the sporting event or recreational activity, Jamaicans like to be in a group, and the larger the group, the better.

Jamaican Athletes and Olympians

From the period immediately following World War II, Jamaican track-and-field athletes have been world champions at the international level, including the Olympics. Some of these Olympic athletes include Herb McKenley, Donald Quarrie, Arthur Wint, and Merlene Ottey. In 1980, Ottey made history by becoming the first female athlete from Jamaica to win an Olympic medal. In the 1996 Olympics, Jamaica ranked in the top five in the world in the number of medals won per capita of population.

The Teen Scene

Although they also involve themselves in such sports as soccer and cricket, many Jamaican teens prefer to hang out with their friends at shopping centers across the island. In groups, they attend parties, clubs, and teen-centered stage performances, where artists perform their most popular songs. Often the majority of the audience is made up of teenagers. Currently, these teens prefer dancehall music. In the evenings, especially on weekends, nightclubs are filled to capacity with eager customers who enjoy music, beverages, and the company of friends. Kingston is the most popular clubbing scene.

Jamaican teenagers also enjoy attending music festivals that showcase the diverse music culture of Jamaica. Established in 1993, Reggae Sumfest is one of the major music festivals held annually in Jamaica. The festival features performances from international and local reggae artists. Each year, crowds of up to 50,000 people gather at Montego Bay to enjoy the music and atmosphere of the festival, which lasts for several days. Such festivals allow Jamaicans to interact with other reggae music enthusiasts from around the world.

Below: **These Rastafarian Jamaicans are enjoying a day out in Kingston.**

Cinema

Jamaica is better known as a location for feature films and television programs than as a producer of its own cinema. Since the 1950s, Jamaica has provided the setting for a wide range of feature films. Along the way, Jamaicans have developed a range of professional skills on both sides of the camera. Jamaicans have produced a number of local films, some successful and others less so. The first feature-length movie made entirely by a Jamaican for local and international release was *The Harder They Come* (1972). This film, which starred Jamaican-born actor and musician Jimmy Cliff, has been playing steadily in Jamaica's cinemas, on Jamaican television channels, and around the world since its release. Other Jamaican efforts at cinematic productions are *Children of Babylon*, *Countryman*, *Lunatic*, *Third World Cop,* and *Rude Bwoy* (Boy). Many of these films have not had the same level of success as *The Harder They Come*. Another local production that has had some level of success both locally and internationally is the nighttime drama series *Royal Palm Estate*.

Above: **A scene from the James Bond film** *A View to a Kill* **featuring Jamaican-born actress Grace Jones** *(far right).*

Food

Traditional Cuisine

Traditional Jamaican dishes are often highly seasoned. The preferred seasonings are salt, black pepper, thyme, onions, ginger, pimento (allspice), garlic, and hot peppers. There are regional favorites and personal differences in meal preparation. However, certain meals and foodstuffs are the favorites of most people in Jamaica.

At the top of this list is ackee and saltfish, the national dish. Ackee is a bright red fruit with yellow flesh and a few seeds inside. The fish that is usually used in this dish is heavily salted cod. Ackee and saltfish is normally a breakfast meal and is often prepared for Sunday breakfast with other foods, such as bananas, yams, potatoes, and dumplings. Other traditional side dishes are hardough bread, fried or roasted breadfruit, Johnny cakes, and fried bammies. Hardough bread is a heavy white bread in which a large amount of lard is used instead of butter or margarine. Bammy is a round flat cake made from dried cassava, a staple food of the Taino. Johnny cakes are made with a dough of flour and water with pinches of salt and baking powder that is kneaded into round balls and fried.

Left: The ackee fruit is poisonous when unripe. When it reaches maturity, the fruit opens up, and the yellow flesh inside can be cooked and eaten.

TAINO INFLUENCE

The earliest settlers of Jamaica, the Taino, brought a special soup called "pepper pot" to Jamaican cuisine. This soup is made with a lot of pepper as well as a variety of meats. Taino influence also extends to other parts of present-day Jamaican culture.

Immigrant Influences

The traditional recipes and ways of cooking are still widely practiced; however, other kinds of cooking have also been introduced into the Jamaican kitchen. The East Indian and Chinese immigrants brought their own styles of cooking, food, and seasonings from their countries of origin to Jamaica. One of the most popular local dishes, curry goat, is commonly thought of as a Jamaican dish. The East Indians, however, initially introduced it to the island.

Below: Jamaica's bountiful tropical fruits are used to prepare delicious desserts. Some of these fruits, such as coconuts and breadfruit, are not native to the island but were brought to Jamaica from other parts of the world.

Jerk Meat

A characteristically Jamaican food is jerk meat, which can be made from pork, chicken, or fish. The meat is first marinated in a strong-tasting mixture of various herbs and spices, including pepper, thyme, nutmeg, cinnamon, and pimento. Then it is cooked over a pit of burning pimento wood and coals. Jerk meat marinades vary from cook to cook, and some may consist of thirty or more herbs and spices. Because the meat is wrapped with leaves before it is placed over the fire, the process of slowly cooking the meat in its own juices gives jerk meat its unusual tenderness. Today, Jamaican jerk meat is sold not only in Jamaica but in other countries as well.

A CLOSER LOOK AT JAMAICA

Independent Jamaica is a very young nation. The history of the land, however, extends over 1,400 years, beginning with its first inhabitants, the Taino. The Europeans, most notably the Spanish and the English, and the Africans who arrived as slaves for the sugar plantations of the island have all left indelible marks that are unmistakable to the eye of any visitor. Other groups of people have also made Jamaica their homeland, and their cultures have been accepted and assimilated into the Jamaican society to create a unique blend of many people in one. Jamaica's motto, "Out of Many, One People," reflects the island's multiculturalism.

Below: **Jamaican musicians perform along the banks of Rio Grande in the parish of Portland.**

From its folklorists and folklores to its unique historical facts and events, the story of Jamaica is truly vibrant and dynamic. Jamaican reggae music and Rastafarianism are known the world over. The country also honors its national heroes who helped in the fight against slavery and eventually achieved emancipation. Tourists from all over the world visit the island each year to indulge in the sun and sandy beaches of Jamaica and to experience the cheerful, outgoing nature of the Jamaican people.

Opposite: **Ocho Rios is a popular tourist destination. Many colorful street characters entertain visitors there.**

The Blue Mountains

The Blue Mountains form the best-known mountain range in Jamaica. The Blue Mountains and John Crow Mountains spread over three parishes — St. Andrew, St. Thomas, and Portland — in eastern Jamaica. Beneath the thick canopy of vegetation lie scenic waterfalls, pristine lagoons, rivers, and a multitude of flora and fauna.

Thick forests covered these mountains when Columbus first stepped on the island in 1494. Since then, however, much of the forestland has been cleared to make way for the country's increasing population and economic demands. The greatest species diversity in the Caribbean can be found here. Many of the plant and animal species here cannot be found elsewhere in the world. The mountains are also home to the *Papilio homerus*, which is the world's second-largest butterfly.

In 1993, the Blue Mountain and John Crow Mountain National Park was established to protect these areas from deforestation and to prevent the diverse flora and fauna from becoming extinct. The national park covers an area of 196,775 acres (79,666 hectares). The rivers of the Blue and John Crow Mountains supply water for the Kingston area and for several towns within and around the mountain ranges.

HIKING IN THE BLUE MOUNTAINS

Hiking to the Blue Mountain peak is very popular among local and foreign people. The peak of the mountain stands at 7,402 feet (2,256 m) high. Hikers usually start their 7-mile (11-km) journey while it is still dark so they reach the peak in time to watch the sunrise. From the Blue Mountain peak, it is possible to see Cuba on a clear day.

Below: The Blue Mountains gained their name from the dense greenish blue vegetation that covers most of their surfaces.

Blue Mountain Coffee

The coffee plant is not native to Jamaica. It was first brought to the island in 1728 by Sir Nicholas Lawes, the Jamaican governor at the time. Lawes had obtained the coffee seedlings from the island of Martinique, which lies just north of Trinidad and Tobago. The coffee seedlings thrived in the high altitudes of the Blue Mountains, and soon, large areas of land on the slopes of the Blue Mountains were cleared to set up coffee plantations. Coffee became a major export crop for Jamaica.

Only coffee grown in selected areas of the Blue Mountains can be labeled Jamaican Blue Mountain Coffee, a popular gourmet coffee. To maintain the high quality of Jamaican Blue Mountain Coffee, the Coffee Industry Board was established in 1950. It has set strict standards for the cultivation, processing, and export of Jamaican Blue Mountain Coffee. Today, between 85 and 90 percent of the island's coffee exports are sold to Japan.

Above: **This machine processes Jamaican Blue Mountain coffee.**

Buccaneers and Pirates

Jamaica has a rich history of relations with buccaneers and pirates. Movies have been made about pirates who traveled the Caribbean Sea and used Port Royal in Jamaica as the base of their operations and a place to spend their loot.

Buccaneers

Buccaneers first appeared after the Spanish occupation of the Caribbean. Driven by the need to colonize other territories, mainly to capture Spanish lands, other Europeans, such as the Portuguese, English, French, and Dutch, urged individual captains, or buccaneers, to fight against the Spanish. In the 1500s, Jamaica became an ideal base for operations from which the buccaneers could attack Spanish ships in the Caribbean. Encouraged by Queen Elizabeth I, Francis Drake led attacks on ships and towns.

Before long, however, the buccaneers grew into a powerful and ruthless force that the English Crown could not control. They raided far and wide and were feared throughout the Caribbean. These buccaneers then turned to privateering. Privateers were allowed to keep a portion of the loot from the ships they raided.

Above: Henry Morgan is probably the most famous of Port Royal's buccaneers. In 1670, he captured the Spanish city of Panama, where he took 100,000 English pounds in riches. Morgan was only charged for his actions in an English court of law when fighting between England and Spain ceased. By 1673, however, King Charles II knighted Morgan for his bravery, and Sir Henry Morgan later became the lieutenant governor of Jamaica.

Left: This drawing shows ships under the command of buccaneer Henry Morgan attacking the Venezuelan city of Maracaibo.

Pirates

After England made peace with its rivals, the buccaneers were regarded as pirates. The word "pirate" simply means "one who robs or plunders on the sea." Pirates, therefore, added to the colony's problems, and the English government did much to get rid of them. Several pirates rose to fame for their cruelty, daring, and occasionally, their flamboyant ways. Edward Teach, also known as "Blackbeard," was an English pirate active from 1716 to 1718. To terrorize his victims, Teach often wore burning fuses in his uncombed beard and hair. He went further to inflict his cruelty on not only his prisoners, but also his own crew. Teach was finally killed in a battle against the British. Another pirate was "Calico Jack" Rackham, popularly known for his love of calico underwear. Like many pirates before him, he was captured and executed. His body was hung in an iron frame on a small cay off Port Royal. The cay is still called Rackham's Cay.

"WICKED" CITY

Due to the influence of the buccaneers and their wealth from raids on the sea, Port Royal became a wealthy and prosperous port city. Because thieves, prostitutes, and criminals of all types also reportedly inhabited it, Port Royal had a bad reputation.

Cultural Icon of Jamaica

Louise Bennett-Coverley, folklorist and gifted poet, has been one of Jamaica's most prolific cultural icons. Over the years, she contributed significantly to the development of Jamaica's language, poetry, and drama. On the stage, however, she made a major contribution. She brought attention and appreciation for patois, the dialect that most Jamaicans speak, and carved a place for herself in the nation's cultural history. In addition to national acclaim, she became widely known in the United Kingdom and Canada.

Poetry

Born in 1919, Louise Bennett-Coverley began writing poetry in her teens. She became known as Miss Lou, and through her work, she still serves as an ambassador of Jamaican culture. She

Left: **Louise Bennett-Coverley is best known for her research and folklore creations for the Jamaican stage that helped save much Jamaican folk material from extinction. Many of her works are in published form, including poems, songs, and tales of Anancy the spider. In 2001, Bennett-Coverley was awarded the Order of Merit for her remarkable work in promoting Jamaican arts and culture.**

has appeared in humorous leading roles in several Jamaican pantomimes and television shows. The popular television show *Ring Ding*, especially, became a hugely effective medium through which Jamaican folklore and folksongs were preserved and passed on to children. Many Jamaicans grew up on this program and still remember fondly the antics of Miss Lou and Mas Eric, her husband. Miss Lou, however, is more than a comedian and poet. A keen observer and commentator on the major social issues of the time, Miss Lou conveyed her views with wit and humor.

Above: **Learning the poems and stories of "Miss Lou" is part of the school curriculum in Jamaica. Much of her work has been published, most notably** *Jamaica Labrish* **(1966) and** *Anancy and Miss Lou* **(1979).**

Honors

Jamaican cultural life today owes much to Louise Bennett-Coverley's contributions. For her work, she has been honored with a host of titles, including the Member of the Order of the British Empire awarded by Queen Elizabeth II in 1961; the Musgrave Gold and Silver Medals given by the Institute of Jamaica; the Norman Manley Award of Excellence; and in 1974, a Member of the Order of Jamaica, which entitled her to be addressed as "the Honorable Louise Bennett-Coverley."

The Great Port Royal Earthquake

In the seventeenth century, Port Royal was a flourishing trading post of great economic importance to the English. Port Royal also had a reputation for being the "wickedest city in the world" because it was the center of privateering activities in the Caribbean. Brothels, gambling houses, and drinking dens lined the streets of the town.

At 11:40 A.M. on June 7, 1692, a large, destructive earthquake shook the town. In just a matter of a few seconds, an estimated 2,000 people were killed. In the days following the earthquake, a further 3,000 citizens died of injuries and diseases. The events of that day brought the end of Port Royal's fame.

Port Royal's residents were killed by falling buildings, buried as the earth shifted, or dragged out to sea in the tidal wave that followed the shocks. Others died from the many epidemics that spread right after the earthquake. Most of the ships in the harbor were also destroyed. Part of the town sank into the sea and can still be seen on sunny, cloudless days when the sea is calm. Port Royal has never returned to its days of wealth and fame.

Below: **This artillery storehouse, called the "Giddy House" at Fort Charles in Port Royal, was tilted at an angle of 35° in an earthquake that hit Port Royal in 1907. It has been converted into a tourist attraction.**

After the earthquake, many theories surfaced concerning the reasons for its occurrence. The reason that all the people in 1692 agreed upon was that the earthquake was a punishment of the citizens of Port Royal for their wickedness and for not maintaining God's commandments. Although the earthquake was felt islandwide and damaged other towns, the devastation at Port Royal was unmatched elsewhere. It was, therefore, seen as a sign of God's wrath on the people of Port Royal. In a gesture to appease God and to ask for his forgiveness, church services and prayer meetings were held across the island with periods of mourning officially sanctioned by the governor.

Through the centuries, the town suffered more disasters, including fire, hurricanes, and earthquakes. The most serious was the earthquake of 1907, in which buildings and property worth millions of dollars were destroyed.

Above: **Today, Port Royal is full of cruise ships and ferries. The national disaster management headquarters, the Office of Disaster Preparedness and Emergency Management (ODPEM) organizes activities in the month of June to educate the people of Jamaica about preparing for events such as earthquakes.**

Independence Day

On the night of August 5, 1962, all 35,000 seats in the newly constructed National Stadium of Kingston were filled with Jamaicans eagerly awaiting the arrival of the country's independence. On the stroke of midnight, the Union Jack, the flag of the United Kingdom, was lowered. The Jamaican flag was raised in its place, and the Jamaican anthem was played and heard for the first time. With that ceremony, which ended with a fireworks display, Jamaica became a free and autonomous member of the British Commonwealth of Nations.

Jamaica's independence was celebrated over the next two days, and on the second day, August 7, Jamaica's first parliamentary session was held. Jamaica's first prime minister, Alexander Bustamante, received the constitutional documents from Princess Margaret, who attended the ceremony for her sister, Queen Elizabeth II.

Below: **Princess Margaret of England attended the first Independence Day celebration in Jamaica.**

Forty Years of Independence

In 2002, Jamaica celebrated its fortieth year as an independent nation. Organization for the year's celebrations began early, with events kicking off in July. The Jamaica Festival events included the Schools' and Adult Festival competitions; the Popular Song Competition (formerly known as the Festival Song Competition) in which individuals compete for the coveted top prize for most popular song title; the Festival Queen Competition; and other local events such as the crowning of the Farm Queen during the Denbigh Agricultural Show. The Independence Day float parade, once a common feature of the independence celebrations in Jamaica, was reintroduced.

The independence festivities also included the opening of the new Emancipation Park, a welcomed addition to the busy Kingston scene. Street dances, parades, fireworks, and church services were all a part of the mass celebration of Jamaica's fortieth year of independence. These celebrations extended well beyond the Jamaican shores as Jamaican consulates in overseas territories held their own celebrations and Jamaican communities across the world celebrated along with their relatives and friends in Jamaica.

Above: **These girls are part of the choir that performed at the National Stadium of Kingston during Jamaica's first Independence Day celebration in 1962.**

"King" Sugar

Sugar became the main product of the Jamaican economy beginning with the English occupation of the island. Faced with the economic decline of tobacco on the world market, the English had to find a viable alternative in order to fill the requirements of the new colony — to become a producer of tropical products for the English people. The one product found most suited to the soil and climate of Jamaica that could be produced on a large scale was sugar.

Sugar Plantations

Sugar plantations were usually large-scale holdings ranging from a few hundred to thousands of acres (ha) of land. A sugar plantation aimed at being self-sufficient, so land was provided for growing timber for fuel, for pasture, and of course, for planting sugarcane. About one-third of the prime plantation land was under sugar cultivation. On the grounds were the buildings required for sugarcane processing: the mill house, boiling house, trash house, distilling house, curing house, and still house. The other buildings on the plantation included the "great house," which was the residence of the owner if he lived on the plantation. If the owner did not live in Jamaica, usually an attorney or an overseer occupied the house.

Below: This illustration shows the interior of an eighteenth-century sugarcane boiling house in Jamaica.

Left: This tractor on a sugar plantation is loading sugarcane for processing. Sugarcane juice and molasses are also used in distilling houses for manufacturing rum.

Producing Sugar

Each crop year began in August. During this time, called the dead season, the cane fields were weeded, cleared, and made ready for the new crop. The hardest work was done by the youngest and strongest slaves. By the beginning of November, cane fields were reaped. Crop time began then and continued until July. The cane was crushed at the mill, the juice sent to the boiling house, and the trash sent to the trash house to be used as fuel. In the boiling house, the liquid was passed through several copper boilers. When the liquid began to crystallize in the hottest copper boiler, it was put in hogsheads, or barrels. The remaining molasses drained through tiny holes made in the hogsheads. The substance left inside the hogsheads was called "muscovado" sugar. It was sent to England for processing and sold on the market.

Sugar Production in Present-Day Jamaica

Sugar is still one of the chief crops in Jamaica. This industry, however, has faced many problems in the past few years. Low yields and inefficient production techniques have placed it in secondary importance to other industries, such as tourism, Jamaica's main economic activity. Sugar industry officials blame heavy rainfall, a decline in quality, and illegal cane field burning as factors that contributed to the decline of Jamaica's 2002 sugar crop yield.

SUGAR MONOPOLY

Sugar production needed a lot of land and labor. With the growing importance of the crop to the economy, the main interests of the colonialists lay in establishing large sugar plantations. Small-scale farmers diminished in number as their lands came under the ownership of the powerful sugar planters.

Kingston

Kingston is Jamaica's capital city and covers an area of less than 8.5 square miles (22 square km). The city is also the country's smallest and most crowded parish. The population density in Kingston is 4,760 persons per square mile (12,500 per square km).

History

Kingston developed after Port Royal was destroyed by an earthquake in 1692 and then a fire in 1703. Port Royal residents began to move across the harbor, and Kingston soon replaced Port Royal as Jamaica's main port. In 1713, Kingston was made a parish, and by the end of the eighteenth century, more than 3,000 brick homes had been built in the area. Kingston became a city in 1802.

Kingston developed rapidly to become the country's trade center. The growth in business at the Kingston Harbor attracted more and more Jamaicans, and soon, the residents of Kingston began to spill over into St. Andrew, a neighboring parish. The building of roads and houses in Kingston roughly followed a gridlike pattern, and except for a few additions, the original development pattern of the city has remained.

A NEW CAPITAL

Spanish Town was the capital of Jamaica until the mid-1700s, when Admiral Charles Knowles, then the governor of Jamaica, tried to declare Kingston the new capital. The king of England rejected the admiral's call, as did the people of Spanish Town. Despite the opposition, Kingston was made the new capital a few years later.

Below: Kingston's horizon includes a breathtaking view of the Blue Mountains.

Kingston Today

Located in southeastern Jamaica, Kingston continues to develop in all directions, except the south. Industrial and residential districts are growing eastward from Kingston. To the north, a residential area is expanding into St. Andrew. To the west, another residential area is expanding into Portmore, St. Catherine. Residential developments are especially welcome in Kingston because they provide homes for Jamaicans who have to work in Kingston and cannot find satisfactory housing in the area. For this reason, Portmore is sometimes called a dormitory residential area.

As Kingston expanded, the Knutsford Park Race Track gave way to the development of New Kingston, which is a large commercial center. Development of New Kingston started in the mid-1960s, and today, the area bears little resemblance to the dust bowl that existed after the track closed. Dominating the skyline in New Kingston are high-rise buildings, which house various businesses, banks, and large hotels, including Hilton Kingston, Wyndham, and Pegasus. Complementing the commercial developments in New Kingston are also numerous food and entertainment establishments, which include a supermarket, a cinema, shopping malls, nightclubs, and fast-food outlets.

Above: Tucked away from the city's main commercial area, surburban Kingston has many quiet and serene residential neighborhoods.

ST. ANDREW'S "PENS"

During the 1700s, wealthy residents in Kingston began buying old "pens" in St. Andrew parish. "Pen" referred to a farm where livestock was kept. Until recently, many areas in St. Andrew were still called pens. A few years ago, these pens were renamed "gardens."

Legends and Folktales

Jamaica's oral traditions originated from African slaves and date as far back as the seventeenth century. Today, legends and folktales play a very important part in Jamaica's culture. Through these stories, handed down from generation to generation by word of mouth, children learn of the strength and resistance activities of slaves, the supernatural strength of their heroes, and the cunning of their forefathers.

Forces and Figures

Jamaican folklore includes two types of spiritual elements or characters. Obeah is believed to have originated from the Southern Caribbean region. It has been described as both a system of belief and a figure that uses sorcery or magic rituals. According to believers, obeah can perform both good and evil deeds, but it is more likely to cause trouble. As a result, believers are always mindful not to tempt obeah by saying out loud how fortunate or how happy they are, for fear that obeah will change the situation. Jumbies are said to be the spirits of dead people who do not want to leave. Jumbies are believed to live in people's houses and can be either good or evil.

ANANCY STORIES

Many Jamaican folktales are told about Anancy the spider, a character with African origins. The stories are used as parables to teach lessons to Jamaican children. Folktales about Anancy present him as small and weak, but he beats his bigger and stronger opponents by using brainpower and wit.

Left: **The Rose Hall Estate near Montego Bay was owned by Annie Palmer, who was also known as the "White Witch of Rose Hall." She was said to be the most cruel female slave owner who ever lived. Legend has it that she killed her husbands by poisoning them and also practiced the black arts. She was eventually killed by her own slaves.**

Left: **The tombstone of Lewis Galdy, who is known as "the man who was buried twice," is in Port Royal. Legend has it that during the 1692 earthquake in Port Royal, Lewis Galdy dropped into a crack in the ground and was swallowed whole. He was spat out of the hole during an aftershock and thrown into the sea. He swam to safety and went on to live for many more years.**

Other legends involve the supernatural abilities of common people or historical figures of Jamaica. For example, Nanny of Maroons, Jamaica's only female National Hero, is represented in stories as a fearless warrior who uses supernatural powers to defeat British soldiers.

In Recent Years

To many Jamaicans, it is important to maintain the oral storytelling tradition and to compile and publish Jamaican folktales. Amina Blackwood Meeks, the founder of Jack Mandora, the Storytelling Association of Jamaica, keeps Jamaica's folklore alive through storytelling shows and workshops. Children are also told these stories by their parents and grandparents. Many stories have been published and are distributed in schools, where special periods are often devoted to reading these books. Folklorists such as Louise Bennett-Coverley have helped in this endeavor by fostering a love and respect for Jamaica's folktales. Contemporary authors include Martha W. Beckwith, Pamela C. Smith, and Daryl C. Dance.

The Maroons

When the English arrived to seize Jamaica from the Spanish in 1655, the Spanish escaped to the neighboring island of Cuba with all their possessions. Before the Spanish left, they freed their African slaves, who took shelter in the forests of the Blue Mountains. This group of freed slaves was given the name "Maroons," which originates from a Spanish word meaning "wild" or "untamed." The Maroons continued to defy English possession of the island for many years by raiding English plantations and freeing slaves.

In the 1700s, Maroon populations grew significantly with the addition of runaway slaves from plantations across the island. The Maroons sought to live freely and settled in the mountains, where they created villages far away from their oppressors at the sugar plantations. Over time, Maroon settlement became clearly divided and consisted of the Windward and the Leeward Maroons. The Windward Maroons dominated eastern Jamaica, while the Leeward Maroons took the island's west.

Below: **The Maroons in the town of Accompong celebrate their annual Maroon Festival. This event is held on January 6 to commemorate the signing of a peace treaty betweeen the leaders of the Maroons and the English.**

Above: A **festive procession involving the entire town is one of the events held as part of the annual Maroon Festival.**

Although the Maroons settled far away from the sugar plantations to avoid recapture by British authorities, the distance that separated the Maroons and the planters did little to reduce the number of conflicts between them. They fought many small battles and two all-out wars — the First and Second Maroon Wars. After the Second Maroon War, the Leeward Maroons in Trelawny were deported to Nova Scotia in Canada and later to Sierra Leone in Africa.

The Maroons Today

Groups of Maroons still exist today, holding onto their cultural practices and history. Each year, they celebrate the signing of the 1739 treaty and the recognition of Nanny of the Maroons as one of Jamaica's National Heroes. Festivals are held each year to celebrate aspects of Maroon culture. Maroons who have moved to other parts of the world also attend the festivals. In addition, there are efforts to attract tourists and to promote the Maroon culture throughout the island and the wider international community.

The National Heroes

Since 1962, when Jamaica celebrated its independence, distinguished individuals have been selected from throughout the nation's history to form a group known and honored as Jamaica's National Heroes. The Order of National Hero of Jamaica was created in 1965.

The first National Heroes, named in 1969, were Paul Bogle, George William Gordon, and Marcus Mosiah Garvey. A farmer and a preacher, Bogle is best remembered for leading the 1865 Morant Bay Rebellion. Gordon was hanged for his alleged role in the Morant Bay Rebellion. He was also once a member of the House of Assembly. Garvey is honored for founding the Universal Negro Improvement Association (UNIA).

In 1973, Alexander Bustamante and Norman Washington Manley were declared National Heroes. Bustamante and Manley were founders of the two main political parties that played important roles in the events leading up to Jamaica's independence from the British.

Below: **Smartly dressed guards parade at the entrance to Heroes Park, which houses memorials to Jamaica's National Heroes.**

In 1975, two more heroes — Sam Sharpe and Nanny of the Maroons — were named. Both lived during the period of slavery in Jamaica, hated slavery, and tried in separate ways to end the system that enslaved them. The only female National Hero, Nanny was a leader of the Windward Maroons and forged a fierce resistance movement against slavery from the town named after her, Nanny Town, in the parish of Portland. Under Nanny, who was an exceptional military leader, the Windward Maroons raided plantations, set slaves free, and lived relatively free lives in the hills of the Blue Mountains. Nanny died in the 1750s.

Sharpe, on the other hand, did not think that violence was necessary for the slaves to achieve freedom. A preacher, he chose, instead, to ask the slaves to refuse to do any work on Christmas Day of 1831. This was to have been the first step in his long-term plans for attaining freedom for the slaves. On Christmas Eve, however, some of his followers rebelled and urged more to join them. Plantation buildings were destroyed and sugarcane fields torched as a result of the rebellion, which gave the government the excuse "to shoot and murder the people without mercy." On May 23, 1832, Sharpe was executed, although he himself was not responsible for the mayhem that the slaves caused.

Above: **A memorial to Marcus Mosiah Garvey stands at Heroes Park in Kingston to honor the man whose teachings are the basis of the Rastafarian movement in Jamaica. Born in 1887, he is also known for his "Back to Africa" movement, which called for all people of African descent to return to their ancestral home, Ethiopia.**

Pollution in the Kingston Harbor

Kingston Harbor is the world's seventh-largest natural harbor. Formerly a major nursery farming fifteen species of fish, Kingston Harbor used to produce about 800,000 pounds (362,880 kilograms) of edible fish each year. Today, it is a sanctuary, or haven, for birds, and some reptiles, shrimp, oysters, and dolphins are also known to live near the harbor.

The Problem

Marine life in Kingston Harbor largely has been dead for decades, the result of effluents and other stifling material that enter the water. For instance, it is estimated that 20 million gallons (76 million liters) of untreated sewage enter the harbor on a daily basis. In addition, tons of sediment accumulate each year. Chemicals and other substances from farming and industry also reach the harbor from runoff via rivers and gullies. High levels of heavy metals, such as lead, arsenic, and mercury, are found in the fish in the harbor. Increasing levels of pesticides were also found in the harbor's water and fish, posing a potential health hazard for

Below: **An artist records an impression of the Kingston Harbor in the eighteenth century.**

birds, animals, and humans who consume the fish. In recent years, the Jamaican government has conducted dredging operations in the Kingston Harbor. The process of dredging requires the use of large machinery to scoop up materials from the bottom of the harbor. Dredging the Kingston Harbor is required to clear the waters for vessels entering the harbor. This procedure, however, is unpopular among environmentalists, who fear that it might cause damage to Jamaica's beautiful coral reefs.

Above: **The Kingston Harbor is considered extremely hazardous for swimming because of the rising levels of pollutants in the water.**

Future of the Kingston Harbor

In recent years, the Jamaican government has worked with international organizations such as The World Bank, the U.S. Agency for International Development (USAID), and the United Nations Environment Program to reduce the pollution levels in the Kingston Harbor. For example, the existing sewage treatment plants are inadequate and need to be updated. The Jamaican government also set up the National Environment and Planning Agency (NEPA) in 2001 to address the worsening pollution levels in the Kingston Harbor. Any improvements, however, will take a long time to implement.

Rastafarians

Rastafarianism is a religion that was created in twentieth-century Jamaica. Like many other religions, Rastafarianism includes different sects. Among them are the Nyabinghi Order, the Bobo Shanti, and the Twelve Tribes of Israel.

In the 1930s, Marcus Mosiah Garvey, a Jamaican black nationalist, developed a set of teachings, which became the foundation of Rastafarianism. Garvey's teachings principally urged black people to empower themselves and also to return to Ethiopia in Africa, the homeland of their ancestors, where they belonged and could lead a better life. Earlier, in 1914, Garvey also founded the Universal Negro Improvement Association (UNIA). Garvey's cause appealed to many Jamaicans who felt oppressed in their own homeland under the rule of the British.

Many Rastafarians believe that former emperor of Ethiopia Halie Selassie is the black messiah, the savior of all black people who have been forced to live under white oppressors. As a result, Rastafarians also believe that Ethiopia is the Promised Land. Before Haile Selassie was crowned in 1930, his name was Ras Tafari. Followers of Garvey adopted Selassie's precoronation name: *Ras*, meaning "prince" and *Tafari*, meaning "to be feared."

Above: **Many Rastafarians adopted dreadlocks while in the hill country in Jamaica, where the movement developed its early characteristics.**

DREADLOCKS

Rastafarians from all sects adopt a common hairstyle known as dreadlocks. Dreadlocks are grown as a sign of devotion to Jah, the holy God of Rastafarianism. Because dreadlocks take a long time to grow, a change of hairstyle is impossible without first shaving off the dreadlocks.

Left: **Rastafarians create carvings such as these for sale.**

Rastafarian Communities

Rastafarian communities differ from one another. For instance, in the Nyabinghi Order, elders or priests guide "brethren" and "sistren" (brothers and sisters, often unrelated by blood but related by their religious affiliation), and they observe the Sabbath on Tuesdays. Among their lifestyle habits are a diet of organic products such as grains, legumes, herbs, barks, vegetables, and nonalcoholic products.

Distinctly different and dressed in long robes and tightly wrapped turbans are the Bobo Shanti Rastafarians. They live separately from all other Rastafarians and the rest of society. Their commune is currently based near Bull Bay in the parish of St. Thomas and is operated like a small independent society, a "government within a government." They have their own constitution and reject the lifestyle, values, and mores of the general society for their own, which are based largely on Old Testament teachings. They produce and manufacture their own products, selling brooms and mats to generate income, which benefits the entire commune.

Above: Rastafarians often wear clothes and accessories that bear the colors of the Ethiopian flag: red, yellow, and green.

THE TWELVE TRIBES

The Twelve Tribes of Israel is more liberal than the other two orders. Its members are free to worship in the churches of their choice or within the privacy of their homes. Twelve Tribes members consider themselves to be the descendants of the twelve sons of Jacob and are divided into twelve houses that are determined by the months of their birth.

Reggae Music

Reggae developed from a combination of Jamaican folk music, traditional African rhythms, and U.S. rhythm and blues. Reggae originated from mento, a simple art form. Laborers and Jamaicans with direct Maroon ancestry developed mento in the early years of the twentieth century. Other music forms, such as ska, which evolved in the late 1950s, and rock steady, which is similar to ska but has a slower beat, also influenced reggae music.

In the 1970s, reggae music took the form of music with a message. Groups and individuals used reggae to express messages of politics, religion, or social commentary. People in this war-torn period fully accepted reggae's conscious lyrics. Over the years, the popularity of reggae music increased both locally and internationally. Reggae music not only played on stages and on radio but could also be heard in the films of this period. For example, the music by Jimmy Cliff was featured in the movie *The Harder They Come* (1972).

Below: **Reggae Sunsplash is a concert held annually in Jamaica to showcase reggae artists.**

Robert "Bob" Nesta Marley (1945–1981)

The world of reggae lost its most influential international star when Robert Nesta Marley died in 1981. Initially, Marley was a member of the band The Wailers. Social commentary inspired the band to produce many songs. Band members, including Marley, sought to make their voices heard by writing about Third World issues and also those within the Jamaican society in their songs. "Rebel Music" and "Them Belly Full" are two examples of the band's songs. The former criticized police harassment, while the latter was about poverty and hunger. In late 1974, Marley formed a new group in which he was the lead singer and Judy Mowatt, Marcia Griffiths, and his wife, Rita Marley, were backup singers. They called themselves the I-Threes. The Wailers reunited to perform again by early 1976. The band also began a world tour, which included countries in North America, Europe, and Asia. Perhaps their most meaningful concert of all was the one they gave in Zimbabwe, Africa. Bob Marley was awarded the Order of Merit for his contribution to reggae music in Jamaica.

Above: Bob Marley's funeral service was held in Kingston's National Heroes Arena.

THE BOB MARLEY MUSEUM

Bob Marley's former residence in the parish of Kingston was converted to a museum. Visitors gain insight into the life of Bob Marley and view artifacts, photographs, and writings related to him.

The Slave Trade

With the coming of the Europeans to Jamaica and the development of large sugar plantations, farmers felt a need for a reliable, cheap, and abundant labor supply. Taino laborers were not sufficient. In fact, the Europeans had reduced their numbers drastically by enslaving them and treating them harshly. With the opening of the African coast to trade with the European nations, Africans were quickly seen as a good source of labor for the Jamaican and the wider Caribbean's plantations.

The Middle Passage

Captured from western Africa, slaves were shipped to the Caribbean through a voyage called the "Middle Passage." The slaves on these ships traveling the Middle Passage were chained below deck and only brought up once a day for exercise. Conditions below deck were deplorable; many diseases and epidemics broke out among the slaves. They also suffered from heat stroke and severe undernourishment. Many died as a result of these conditions.

Below: **Slaves were often cruelly chained to posts in a slave hut. Chains prevented the slaves and their children from running away during the night.**

70

Slavery and Emancipation

In Jamaica, slaves were sold first to the Spanish and later to English plantation owners mainly to plant and reap sugar. Newly arrived slaves were put through a process of "seasoning" in which they were supervised by a plantation slave and trained in the work of a Jamaican plantation. Seasoned slaves were placed into various slave occupational groups, such as the house or domestic slaves, the field slaves, and the artisan slaves. The life of a slave was very hard, and many slaves died as result of their harsh work environments.

The first half of the 1800s signaled the beginning of the end of slavery. More and more people grew intensely opposed to slavery. The economic climate also called for the end of slavery because many slaves rebelled against the plantation owners, who found it costly to keep them under control. Additionally, a growing humanitarian movement in England contributed to the end of slavery. The slaves themselves also demanded their freedom through protests and acts of rebellion. As a result of all of these factors, the British Parliament eventually granted slaves full emancipation on August 1, 1838.

SHIPS FROM HELL

The worst conditions in the Middle Passage were experienced between the years of 1650 and 1750 because of the lack of regulations governing the health conditions on these ships. High mortality rates also occurred as a result of deliberate drowning of slaves in order to claim insurance, the killing of rebel slaves, heat stroke, undernourishment, and excessive cruelty.

Tourism

Tourist earnings provided about one-quarter of the country's gross domestic product (GDP) in 1995. Since then, tourism has been supporting an increasingly large part of the Jamaican economy. Today, tourism is Jamaica's largest foreign exchange earner and also the largest employer of the local Jamaican population. About 32,000 Jamaicans are employed in the service industries related to tourism in Jamaica.

The country's tropical climate, exquisite landscapes, and superb beaches attract many thousands of people from all over the world. The main tourist centers in Jamaica are Montego Bay in St. James, Ocho Rios in St. Ann, and Port Antonio in Portland. The resort area of Negril in the parish of Westmoreland is a highly popular tourist destination. Many tourists also visit the museums, clubs, and other historical attractions in the capital city, Kingston. The Jamaica Tourist Board (JTB) is the main marketing agency of the tourist industry in Jamaica.

Below: **The view of Joseph's Cave in Negril is breathtaking. The Jamaican government aims to achieve sustainable tourism in which the tourist sector is balanced between the built, natural, cultural, and human environment.**

Ecotourism in Jamaica

The northern coast of Jamaica has traditionally been the center of tourist activity on the island. Recently, however, Jamaica's southern coast has also grown as a tourist destination because of the growing popularity of nature tourism, or ecotourism, in these areas. Tourists who are more adventurous travel to the southern coast to visit the national parks in these areas and to hike in the Blue Mountains.

Sustainable Tourism

The dramatic growth of the tourist industry in Jamaica has brought problems to the island's natural environment. In order to meet the rising numbers of tourists visiting the island annually, many forest areas and natural habitats on the island are cleared away to build more restaurants, hotels, and shopping centers. The government of Jamaica has now recognized the need to emphasize environmental protection and to create a tourist industry that is environmentally friendly.

Above: **Although Jamaica plays host to thousands of tourists every year, many beaches, such as the one above in Montego Bay, are not overcrowded.**

(1)
From the following
prepare a three column
Book the month Of
1995
a/ B/d - Cash 1580
Bank overdraft
The following paid us
by cheque in each
15% cash discount:
M. Jarrett 900, P. Brown
A. Levin 1800.
Cash sales paid direct
bank #3200
Cash drawings

RELATIONS WITH NORTH AMERICA

Jamaica has had close ties with North America for hundreds of years. Starting with the early settlement of Jamaica by the British, the colony depended on the United States for imported consumer goods. It was not until the twentieth century, however, that the United States and the Caribbean developed closer ties because of the growing U.S. poicy of interventionism and support to smaller nations within its region of influence. Today, the United States is one of Jamaica's chief trading partners. U.S.-Jamaica relations also include cultural exchanges among scholars, athletes, and religious and artistic groups.

Opposite: **The United States has, over the years, granted financial aid to Jamaica to improve the education system on the island.**

Like the United States, Canada has long had close ties with Jamaica and the wider Caribbean. Being a colony of the British as well, Canada served as a supplier of certain items that Jamaicans could not produce on their own during the colonial period. Canada continues to maintain close ties with Jamaica. As members of the Commonwealth of Nations, Canada and Jamaica have developed a close relationship, with Canada supporting Jamaica in many ways. Overall, Jamaican-North American relations are further bolstered by a large and supportive Jamaican immigrant community in both the United States and Canada.

Above: **U.S.-style fast-food outlets, such as this KFC restaurant in Kingston, can be found in many parts of the island.**

Early Relations with the United States

The United States has traditionally maintained close political, commercial, and personal ties with Jamaica. In 1962, when Jamaica attained independence, Prime Minister Alexander Bustamante announced his intention to develop and maintain friendly relations with the United States.

Cuba, Jamaica's closest neighbor in the Caribbean, developed close relations with the Soviet Union, a communist state. The Jamaican government was aware of the strong rivalry that existed between the United States and the Soviet Union, so it rejected a Soviet-styled government.

After Fidel Castro seized power in Cuba, the United States began to pay closer attention to political events in Jamaica. In 1972, the People's National Party (PNP) won the general elections in Jamaica. The new prime minister, Michael Manley, developed close relations with Cuba, much to the disapproval of the United States. Michael Manley also spoke out against Jamaica's traditional economic reliance on the United States and U.S. imperialism. The situation worsened when he openly declared

Left: Jamaican prime minister Michael Manley (*left*) delivers his departing statement as U.S. president George H. Bush (*right*) looks on. The two met in the White House in 1990.

his support for Puerto Rico's attempts to gain independence from the United States. In 1976, Cuba's relations with Jamaica grew closer, and Manley visited Cuba. The following year, Cuban president Fidel Castro visited Jamaica in return and was warmly welcomed by the Jamaican people.

Above: **U.S. president Ronald Reagan (*left*) met Jamaican prime minister Edward Seaga (*right*) at the White House in 1981.**

Relations between the United States and Jamaica improved when Edward Seaga, leader of the Jamaica Labor Party (JLP), became prime minister of Jamaica. In 1980, Prime Minister Seaga relinquished friendly relations with Cuba and began close, cooperative relations with the U.S. administration of President Ronald Reagan. Seaga was the first foreign leader to visit Washington D.C., after Reagan's inauguration in January 1981.

In 1981, U.S. aid to Jamaica increased dramatically. Between 1981 and 1986, Jamaica received about U.S. $125 million a year in aid from the United States. The Reagan administration also made Jamaica a ket part of the Caribbean Basin Initiative (CBI), a program Prime Minister Seaga helped to inspire that gave trade benefits to participating Caribbean countries.

Between 1980 and 1987, Prime Minister Edward Seaga met periodically with President Reagan and other senior U.S. officials. In April 1982, President Reagan became the first U.S. president to visit Jamaica.

Above: **Containerships in Jamaica load cargo bound for export to the United States.**

Economic Relations

Trade relations between Jamaica and the United States are especially robust. The United States is the single largest buyer of Jamaican goods. In 2000, nearly 40 percent of Jamaican exports were sold to the United States, and trade between the two nations amounted to nearly U.S. $2 billion. Today, more than 80 U.S. businesses are represented in Jamaica, and U.S. investments in the country are in excess of U.S. $ 1 billion. Both the U.S. and Jamaican governments have also worked to maintain mutually beneficial trade relations. In 2001, U.S. president George W. Bush went to Quebec, Canada to attend the Summit of the Americas, where he met with leaders of various Caribbean nations. The purpose of the summit was to foster stronger relations between the Caribbean nations, as well as their willingness to cooperate with North America. Since becoming Jamaica's prime minister in 1992, P. J. Patterson has also paid several official visits to Washington, D.C. The Jamaican government fully supports the the founding of the Free Trade Area of the Americas (FTAA).

United States Aid and Assistance

USAID began operating in Jamaica in 1962. Because the island has long been saddled with a host of social and economic problems, USAID has implemented many projects to address them. Strengthening Jamaica's struggling economy, however, remains the most important issue of all. It is the belief and hope of those who represent USAID that developing sustainable economic growth for Jamaica is the key to releasing its people from much of their current hardships. To attain this goal, USAID has taken steps to guide the current Jamaican economy toward diversification, which includes moving away from an overreliance on the country's traditional industries and exploring new export possibilities that are, at once, not detrimental to the island or its people and financially sound. USAID has also implemented projects to reduce population growth, improve health care facilities, and protect the island's natural environment from the negative effects of tourism. In 2002, Jamaica received about U.S. $13 million in development aid under USAID.

IN CASE OF DISASTERS

USAID also operates an Office of Foreign Disaster Assistance that offers technical and financial aid to help Jamaica and other countries in the Caribbean to be more prepared when faced with natural disasters, such as hurricanes and earthquakes.

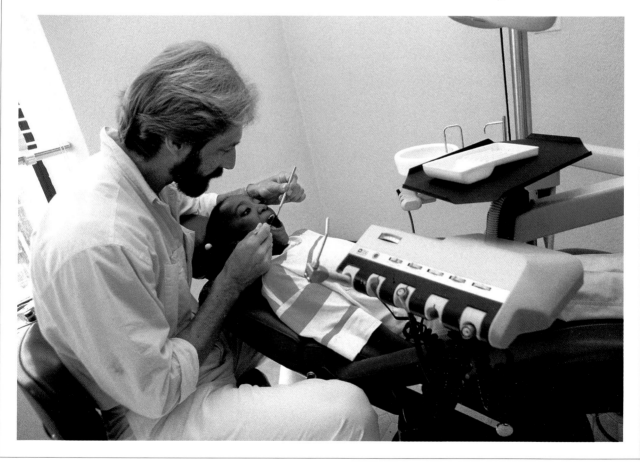

Below: Active in Jamaica since 1962, U.S. Peace Corps volunteers have sought to improve, among other things, health care and sanitation in Jamaica.

Jamaicans in North America

Jamaicans have sought jobs in the United States since the early 1900s. Migration became a matter of economic necessity during the hard economic period when many working-class individuals could not find proper work in Jamaica. The opportunity to work for the U.S. dollar was very appealing, and many Jamaicans used this alternative to maintain their families.

Today, Jamaicans still emigrate principally to the United States. According to figures from the Planning Institute of Jamaica, about 589,700 Jamaicans have settled in the United States, while more than 157,000 Jamaicans have moved to Canada since the 1970s. The Jamaican government also runs several programs in partnership with North American organizations that invite Jamaican applicants for jobs, which may be permanent or temporary, in the United States or Canada. The U.S.-run Hotel Worker Program and the Canadian-run Seasonal Agricultural Workers Program are two such arrangements. Jamaican teachers and highly skilled professionals are also much sought after in North America, where more than 54,280 highly skilled Jamaican professionals have migrated since the 1980s.

COLIN L. POWELL

Colin Powell has been the secretary of state to the U.S. government since 2001. He was born to Jamaican parents who moved from Jamaica to New York. He has been a soldier for thirty-five years and was a four-star general. He was also the twelfth joint chief of staff, which is the highest military position in the U.S. government, and was in charge of the Persian Gulf War.

Below: **Many Jamaicans seek jobs in the service industries of the United States.**

North Americans in Jamaica

Jamaica is a popular destination for many North American tourists. According to the U.S. Department of State, more than 800,000 U.S. tourists visited Jamaica in 2000. Figures from the Jamaica Tourist Board indicate that more than 110,000 Canadians visited Jamaica in 2001 and that they spent an estimated total of U.S. $98 million that year.

As many as 10,000 U.S. citizens live permanently in Jamaica, and among them are many who were born on the island and hold dual citizenship. Apart from those in the diplomatic service, many Americans also live on the island because of their work with U.S. organizations, such as USAID and the Peace Corps, or U.S. businesses that have representative offices in Jamaica, including Coldwell Banker, Cable and Wireless, and Citibank. Both USAID and the Peace Corps have been represented in Jamaica since 1962. Since then, more than 3,300 Peace Corps volunteers have served in the country.

Above: The fun-loving nature of Jamaicans and the hospitality they show their visitors make Jamaica a very popular destination for U.S. tourists.

Partners Against Drug Trafficking

According to the U.S. Drug Enforcement Administration (DEA), large amounts of illicit drugs originating from South America enter the United States via one of the Caribbean states, including Jamaica. As a result, the United States has, in recent years, actively sought Jamaica's cooperation in the fight against drug trafficking. Cocaine, especially, has been increasingly smuggled into the United States via Jamaica. In 2001, more than 3,748 pounds (1,700 kg) of cocaine were seized by Jamaican authorities, who also arrested more than 7,450 drug-related criminals, including 415 foreigners. In 2002, the United States contributed about U.S. $1 million toward improving Jamaica's counternarcotics efforts. Among the main objectives were tightening port and marine security and reducing the Jamaican demand for drugs. In March 2003, the Jamaican Defense Force (JDF) Coast Guard received three Go-Fast boats from the U.S. government as gifts. The boats, worth about U.S. $1.5 million, can attain high speeds and greatly improve the policing power of the JDF Coast Guard.

Above: The headquarters of the Jamaican Coast Guard is located in Port Royal. The funds Jamaica receives from the U.S. government enable the Jamaican authorities to receive advanced training from the U.S. Coast Guard and to purchase new equipment, such as high-speed boats and night-vision goggles, to boost their ability to catch drug smugglers.

Canada and Jamaica

Relations between Canada and Jamaica go back about three hundred years. In 1796, a group of six hundred Maroons was sent to Halifax. Most of them, however, left for Sierra Leone four years later. During World War II, many Jamaicans migrated to join the Canadian Forces. Later, thousands of Jamaican women came to Canada as domestic workers.

Today, Canada's relations with Jamaica include trade and investment links, developmental aid, tourism, and ties of family and friendship to the Jamaican community in Canada. Canada is Jamaica's third most important trading partner, after the United States and the European Union. In 2001, Jamaica sold Can $324.7 million worth of goods to Canada and held about Can $320 million in Canadian investments. Canada began providing aid to Jamaica in 1963, and since then, Jamaica has received about Can $530 million. The Canadian International Development Agency (CIDA) has also promised to improve early childhood education in Jamaica, with a budget of up to Can $5 million between the years of 2001 and 2004.

DONOVAN BAILEY

One of the most famous Jamaican-born athletes in Canada is Donovan Bailey, who was named Canadian Athlete of the Year in 1996. He represented Canada in the 1996 Olympics in Atlanta, where he won the gold medal for the men's 100-meter race, which he ran in 9.84 seconds.

Below: Donovan Bailey (*left*) of Canada, Ato Boldon (*center*) of Trinidad and Tobago, and Maurice Greene (*right*) of the United States compete in the 2001 IAAF World Athletics Championships held in Canada.

Garth Fagan (1940–)

Well-loved choreographer and dance teacher Garth Fagan was born in Jamaica, where he started his dancing career at the National Dance Theater Company of Jamaica (NDTC). Fagan went on to work with various Detroit-based dance companies after he moved to the United States in 1960, and by the late 1960s, began teaching dance at the State University of New York (SUNY). Working most frequently with disadvantaged African American students, he formed, in 1970, an amateur ensemble called The Bottom of the Bucket BUT... Dance Theater. The troupe grew to gain a reputation for its innovative blend of Afro-Caribbean with modern dance styles and, in 1981, was renamed the Bucket Dance Theater. Since 1990, the group has been known as the Garth Fagan Theater. Fagan gained wider national exposure in 1991, when he worked with trumpeter Wynton Marsalis and sculptor Martin Puryear to produce a celebrated artistic work called *Griot New York*. More recently, in 1997, his work in the Broadway musical *The Lion King* won international acclaim and also a Tony award for choreography.

Below: Garth Fagan (*right*) poses for a picture with opera singer Jessie Norman (*left*) at a party. The son of Jamaica's former chief education officer, Fagan has been a Distinguished University Professor at SUNY since 1986.

Harry Belafonte (1927–)

Harry Belafonte was born in Harlem, New York. His mother came from Jamaica, and his father came from the island of Martinique, which is just north of Trinidad and Tobago in the Caribbean sea. When he was eight years old, Belafonte moved to his mother's homeland, where he stayed for several years. In 1940, Belafonte returned to the United States.

Belafonte began his career in entertainment as a stage actor. He studied at Erwin Piscator's Dramatic Workshop and performed with the American Negro Theatre. Belafonte's big break, however, came in 1956, when he released his first album, *Calypso*. The album became the first in the United States to sell over one million copies. Over the years, Belafonte worked on many television and film productions, as well as musical recordings and compositions. *Carmen Jones* (1954), *Buck and the Preacher* (1972), *Prêt-à-Porter* (1994), and *Kansas City* (1996) are just a few of the many movies in which he has starred. In 1987, Belafonte was appointed a Goodwill Ambassador of the United Nations Children's Fund (UNICEF) for his humanitarian work.

Above: **Harry Belafonte (***left***) attended a state dinner hosted by U.S. president Bill Clinton (***right***) at the White House in May 2000.**

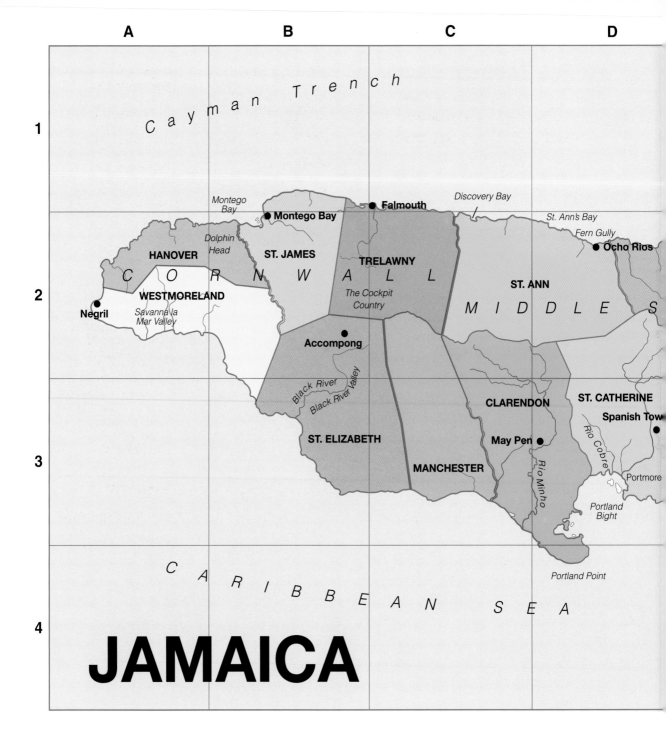

C a y m a n   T r e n c h

1

Montego Bay

● **Montego Bay**   ● **Falmouth**   *Discovery Bay*   *St. Ann's Bay*

Fern Gully

HANOVER   *Dolphin Head*   **ST. JAMES**   **TRELAWNY**   ● **Ocho Rios**

C   O   R   N   W   A   L   L   **ST. ANN**

2   **WESTMORELAND**   *The Cockpit Country*   M   I   D   D   L   E   S

● **Negril**   *Savanna la Mar Valley*

● **Accompong**

Black River

Black River Valley   **CLARENDON**   **ST. CATHERINE**

ST. ELIZABETH   ● **Spanish Tow**

● **May Pen**   *Rio Cobre*

3   **MANCHESTER**   *Rio Minho*   ● Portmore

Portland Bight

Portland Point

C   A   R   I   B   B   E   A   N   S   E   A

4

JAMAICA

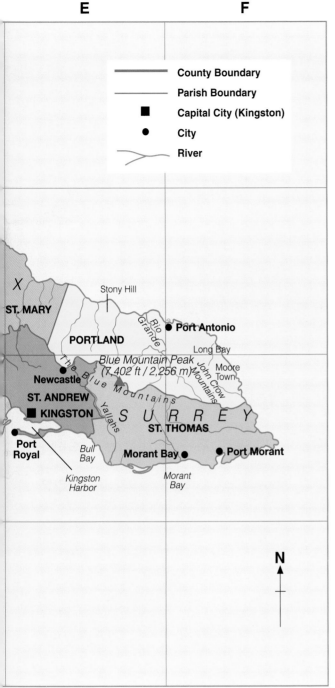

E　　　　F

County Boundary
Parish Boundary
Capital City (Kingston)
City
River

X

ST. MARY

Stony Hill

Rio Grande

PORTLAND

● Port Antonio

Long Bay

Blue Mountain Peak
(7,402 ft / 2,256 m)

The Blue Mountains

John Crow Mountains

Moore Town

Newcastle ●

ST. ANDREW

■ KINGSTON

Yallahs

S U R R E Y

ST. THOMAS

● Port
Royal

Bull
Bay

Morant Bay ●

● Port Morant

Kingston
Harbor

Morant
Bay

N

Accompong B2

Black River B2-B3
Black River Valley
　　B2-B3
Blue Mountain Peak E3
Blue Mountains E3-F3
Bull Bay E3

Caribbean Sea A4-F4
Cayman Trench A1-C1
Clarendon C2-D4
Cockpit Country B2-C3
Cornwall A2-C3

Discovery Bay C2
Dolphin Head B2

Falmouth C1
Fern Gully D2

Hanover A2-B2

John Crow Mountains F3

Kingston E3
Kingston Harbor
　　D3-E3

Long Bay F3

Manchester C2-C3
May Pen D3
Middlesex C2-D3
Montego Bay B2
Moore Town F3
Morant Bay F3

Negril A2
Newcastle E3

Ocho Rios D2

Port Antonio F2
Port Morant F3
Port Royal E3
Portland E2-F3
Portland Bight D3
Portland Point D4
Portmore D3

Rio Grande E2-F3
Rio Cobre D3

St. Andrew D2-E3
St. Ann C2-D2
St. Ann's Bay D2
St. Catherine D2-D3
St. Elizabeth B2-B3
St. James B1-B2
St. Mary D2-E2
St. Thomas E3-F3
Savannah La Mar Valley
　　A2
Spanish Town D3
Stony Hill E2
Surrey E2-F3

Trelawny B1-C2

Westmoreland A2-B3

Yallah's Valley E3

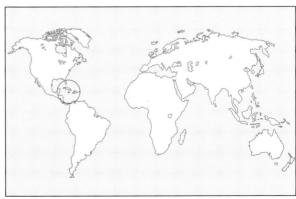

87

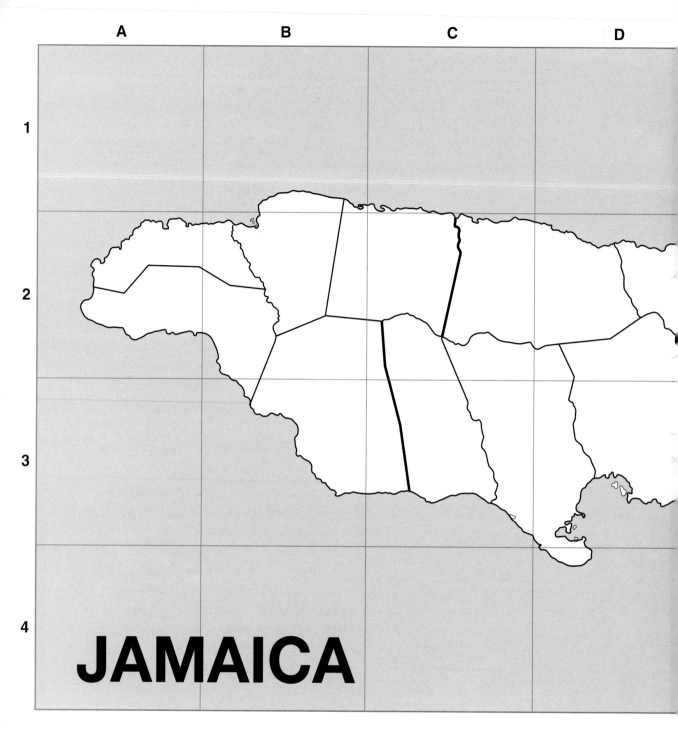

JAMAICA

E   F

N

How Is Your Geography?

Learning to identify the main geographical areas and points of a country can be challenging. Although it may seem difficult at first to memorize the locations and spellings of major cities or the names of mountain ranges, rivers, deserts, lakes, and other prominent physical features, the end result of this effort can be very rewarding. Places you previously did not know existed will suddenly come to life when referred to in world news, whether in newspapers, television reports, other books and reference sources, or on the Internet. This knowledge will make you feel a bit closer to the rest of the world, with its fascinating variety of cultures and physical geography.

This map can be duplicated for use in a classroom. (PLEASE DO NOT WRITE IN THIS BOOK!) Students can then fill in any requested information on their individual map copies. The student can also make a copy of the map and use it as a study tool to practice identifying place names and geographical features on his or her own.

Jamaica at a Glance

Official Name	Jamaica
Capital	Kingston
Nationality	Jamaican
Official Language	English
Other Languages	Patois (Jamaican Creole)
Total Population	2,680,029 (2002 estimate)
Land Area	4,244 square miles (10,991 square km)
Counties	Cornwall, Middlesex, Surrey
Parishes	Clarendon, Hanover, Kingston, Manchester, Portland, St. Andrew, St. Ann, St. Catherine, St. Elizabeth, St. James, St. Mary, St. Thomas, Trelawny, Westmoreland
Highest Point	Blue Mountain 7,402 feet (2,256 m)
Major Rivers	Black River, Rio Cobre, Rio Grande
Head of Government	The prime minister (currently the Hon. Percival James Patterson)
Famous Leader	Norman Washington Manley (1893 – 1969), Alexander Bustamante (1884 – 1977), Michael Manley (1924 – 1997)
Major Religions	Christianity, Jamaican traditional religions
Major Holidays	Good Friday (March/April), Easter (March/April), Independence Day (August), Emancipation Day (August), Christmas (December 25)
Major Imports	Machinery, transport equipment, fuel, food, chemicals
Major Exports	Bauxite, coffee, sugar, bananas, pimento, rum
Currency	Jamaican Dollar (JMD 59.38 = U.S. $1 in 2003)

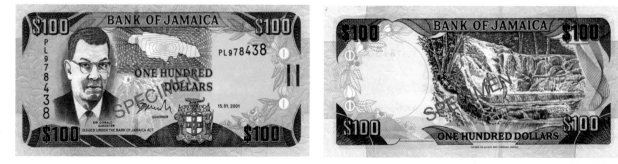

Opposite: **The white egret is a bird commonly seen in Jamaica.**

Glossary

Jamaican Vocabulary

ital (EE-tal): the food and diet of Rastafarians, mostly fruits, nuts, and vegetables.

jumbie (jum-BEE): the spirit of a dead person that refuses to leave the island.

Kumina (koo-MEE-nah): a religious cult that originated in Africa.

Maroons (MER-roons): African slaves who ran away from the sugar plantations and lived in the hills and mountains in Jamaica.

Nyabinghi (NEE-ya-been-yee): a Rastafarian sect.

obeah (oh-BEE-ah): a system of belief that includes sorcery and magic rituals.

patoo (PAH-too): a white owl native to the island of Jamaica.

Pocomania (poh-koh-MAY-nee-ah): a Jamaican religion with African roots.

Taino (tah-EE-no): the first inhabitants of Jamaica, formerly known as Arawaks.

English Vocabulary

acclaim: enthusiastic approval or praise.

arsenic: a grayish white element that is poisonous when heated.

assimilated: brought into conformity with the customs and attitudes of a dominant cultural group.

bipartisan: involving two political parties.

buccaneers: ship captains who preyed on Spanish ships and settlements in the sixteenth and seventeenth centuries.

cassava: a tropical plant with starchy, edible roots.

commune: a close-knit community of people who share common interests.

constitution: the system of principles according to which a state is governed.

culinary: of or relating to the kitchen or cooking.

deplorable: very wretched or bad.

devastated: brought to ruin or desolation by violent action.

dialect: a regional variety of language.

distilling: purifying a liquid by first vaporizing it and then condensing it.

diverse: of different kinds or forms.

effluents: sewage or other liquid wastes that are discharged into a flowing body of water.

emancipation: the act of officially freeing a slave from bondage.

environmentalists: people who work for protection of natural resources from pollution or its effects.

epidemics: diseases that affect many individuals at the same time and spread easily from person to person.

fauna: the animals characteristic of a region, period, or special environment.

fiscal year: an accounting year.

flora: plant or bacterial life characteristic of a region, period, or special environment.

Greater Antilles: a group of islands in the West Indies including Cuba, Hispaniola, Jamaica, and Puerto Rico.

husbandry: the scientific control and management of a branch of farming, especially of domestic animals.

imperialism: the policy of extending the rule of a nation over foreign countries.

inauguration: introduction into public use by some formal ceremony.

indelible: unable to be removed or forgotten.

indentured laborer: a person bound to work for another for a specific period of time.

interventionism: a policy of interfering in the affairs of another state.

jurisdiction: the extent or range of judicial, law enforcement, or other authority.

kaleidoscope: a continually shifting pattern or scene.

mangrove: a tropical tree or shrub that grows near the sea, sends out many prop roots, and forms dense masses important in coastal land building.

marinated: soaked in a savory sauce to enrich flavor or tenderize.

mayhem: random or deliberate violence or damage.

messiah: an expected deliverer or savior.

militia: a body of citizens enrolled for military service, called out occasionally for training but acting as soldiers only in emergencies.

molasses: a thick syrup, usually dark brown, that is produced during the refining of sugar.

mongoose: a slender, ferretlike carnivore, some species of which are noted for their ability to kill cobras.

navigable: deep enough and wide enough to afford passage to ships.

ordained: selected to perform ministerial or holy duty or selected as a pastor or minister in a church.

operettas: short operas, usually of a light and amusing character.

parable: a story that illustrates a moral or a principle.

plantations: agricultural estates usually worked by resident labor.

privateer: the captain of a privately owned ship that is commissioned to fight or harass other ships.

propagate: to cause a plant to multiply by any process of natural reproduction.

quadrille: a square dance of four couples consisting of five parts or movements.

rectify: to correct.

relinquished: gave up.

runoff: the portion of precipitation on land that ultimately reaches a body of water, often with dissolved or suspended material.

sanctioned: approved or allowed.

spurs: ridges or lines of elevation projecting from or subordinate to the main body of a mountain or mountain range.

stifling: killing by depriving of oxygen.

strife: violent and bitter enmity or a struggle or armed conflict.

submerged: under the surface of water or any other enveloping medium; hidden from sight.

subservient: serving or acting in a subordinate or inferior capacity or manner.

suffrage: the right to vote, especially in a political election.

synonymous: expressing or implying the same idea or character.

titular: existing in title only.

vulnerable: open to attack or damage.

More Books to Read

Jamaica. Countries, Faces, and Places series. Mary Berendes (Child's World)

Jamaica. Country Insights series. Alison Brownlie (Raintree/Steck Vaughn Publishers)

Jamaica. Cultures of the World series. Sean Sheehan (Benchmark Books)

Jamaica. Discovering the Caribbean series. Colleen Madonna Flood Williams
   (Mason Crest Publishers)

Jamaica. True Books series. Ann Heinrichs (Children's Press)

Jamaica in Pictures. Visual Geography series. Anne Egan, editor (Lerner)

One Love, One Heart: A History of Reggae. James Haskins (Jump at the Sun)

The Magic Feather: A Jamaican Legend. Legends of the World series. Lisa Rojany, editor
   (Troll Associates)

Videos

Jamaica. AAA Travel Video series. (International Video Corp)

Jamaica: Land of Wood and Water. (Video Visits)

The Jamaica Experience. Lonely Planet series. (Questar)

Web Sites

www.jamaicans.com

www.jis.gov.jm

www.discoverjamaica.com

www.nlj.org.jm/

www.jamaicatravel.com/

Due to the dynamic nature of the Internet, some web sites stay current longer than others. To find additional web sites, use a reliable search engine with one or more of the following keywords to help you locate information about Jamaica: *Bob Marley, dancehall music, hutia, John Crow Mountains, Kingston Harbor, pirates, Rastafarianism, Reggae, Taino.*

Index